I Am Bipolar Manic

iUniverse books may be ordered through booksellers or by contacting:

iUniverse
1663 Liberty Drive
Bloomington, IN 47403
www.iuniverse.com
1-800-Authors (1-800-288-4677)

ISBN: 978-1-4502-8189-8 (pbk)
ISBN: 978-1-4502-8190-4 (cloth)
ISBN: 978-1-4502-8191-1 (ebk)

Library of Congress Control Number: 2010919128

Printed in the United States of America

iUniverse rev. date: 3/24/11

I Am Bipolar Manic

KENNETH WATSON

iUniverse, Inc.
Bloomington

I Am
Bipolar Manic

I consider this a gift from God. I never get depressed.
No thought on suicide. Never had a nightmare.
No thoughts on harming anybody.   Always on a high.
I just have to talk and make people happy.
I feel that I have a super brain now.
Bill Gates couldn't buy my brain. (not that he would want to)

1A

My name is Kenneth Watson and this is my life story. I was born in Burnley Lancashire, England in 1930. I was born to a poor family, but there was lots of love in the home. My Father was a painter of houses and I think his wage when I was 5 was about $6. With that money my Mother had to feed us all and pay all the usual expenses, including a mortgage. I don't know how they did it, I was never hungry. We had gas for lights, and there was no T.V. Things were a bit depressed in the North of England, so my Father moved south to Watford where there was more work. Looking back, I think that was pretty amazing. My Father was not an ambitious man so I wonder who gave him the courage to move 200 miles south. He bought a brand new house 3 bedroom 1 bath $1,200 on a mortgage of course, but what a price. We also had a car, it was a standard 8 and he loved that car.

Almost new and only $200 I don't know how he did it. He might have got a little extra money with the move, but not that much. The only thing I can remember when I was 3 years old, was playing board games with all the relations, this was at Burnley. My Mother had a sister and 2 brothers and we were always getting together with her Mum and Dad and we played lots of games, probably to keep me happy. At that time I was the only child and everybody used to spoil me, But I could hold my own with the games. One of the games I remember was snakes and ladders. (I wonder if they still make it). Another incident I can remember, I think it was Blackpool beach. We were playing cricket and I got too close to the person wielding the bat. I was only 5 and I still have the scar on my mouth. It must have hurt. We didn't mix too much with my Dad's relations except for Albert who lived a couple of streets away, strangely enough in Watford who was married to Edith. Albert was a radio tecknition, eventually to become a T.V. man. My Father's other two brothers, Edwin and Harry who was the youngest and there was Pop the Father. I didn't see much of him either. I think he lived to 91 years. I was 5 and I settled in at the local school, which was Garston. I wasn't there too long and then they moved me to a brand new school called Kingswood. It was much closer to home and I remember having some good times there. We had a lot of kids the same age living round us. We played a lot of street games after school. When my Mother wanted me she would wail like Tarzan of the jungle. The kids used to-laugh, but it didn't worry me. I had to go in to shut up the noise. People probably thought we were getting attacked. In his spare time my Father used to paint pictures in oil. He would copy from a small photograph. He was very good. He should have gone to night school to learn more about art. I still have 3 of his paintings to this day. My brother Chris has the rest. I also did some painting and attended night school later on in life. I can't remember where my paintings went to. Another hobby of my Fathers, was to try and pick 8 draws from the English soccer teams. If he had been lucky he would have been very rich. The most he ever won over a lot of years was about $500 Smoking was his other vice, my Mother too. Of course they had never heard of second hand smoke affecting the kids. My Father had no ambition, he was just content to work for somebody else, I can't ever remember them going out dancing or to a restaurant or a pub. Only when the relations got together. He probably couldn't afford it anyway on his wages. The age of 9 soon came around and of course the war broke out and my Mother shipped me off to Burnley which was a safer place to be when the bombs are dropping. I had to enroll in a school.but it was close to where Grandma lived. You see Watford was only 20 miles from London and they were getting some of the left over bombs from the German bombers on their way home.

2A

Burnley was about 200 miles away and not on the flight path. So it was pretty safe. Eventually my Father got called up in the army and they had him guarding the Italian prisoners of war. He was stationed about 25 miles away but didn't get home much' Long enough to get his wife pregnant. Something he didn't think would happen as I was almost 13 lb. when I was born and did a lot of damage and the Doctor said that my Mother would not be able to have any more children. There is 13 and half years between my brother and I. The early bombardment of London eventually died off and I went back home to stay with my Mother She was alone and probably glad of the company. We would have onion sandwiches for supper and then go to bed. I don't think I have had an onion sandwich since. We had a rationing system which didn't give us much. They even rationed candy. I know the British Army didn't pay much anyway, not like the American Army. I used to love baked potatoes, but my Mother stopped making them. She said I would put a whole weeks supply of butter on one potato. We had a bomb shelter in the garden and we used to go down when the air raid warning siren sounded. The school had a big shelter too, and we all had to go down when the siren sounded, In both of the shelters we would play games to pass away the time. I remember at the school we had one of the old gramophone that you had to wind up. We had the big old records too. It passed the time away when you were down the shelter. It was pretty quiet, you wouldn't think there was a war on. It must have been about 1941 and the bombing started again. I think that was the time that they had come up with their pilotless bombs, could have been a little later. We didn't go down the shelters at home again. We just got under the bed. We figured that if we got a direct hit, it wouldn't make any difference anyway.

The school still made us go down. The bombs that flew themselves were very. scarey. You would hear the engine and all of a sudden the engine would stop, then you had better watch out, because its coming down, and they make big damage. We used to call them doodle bugs I think the real name was VI and V2s. One of these monsters demolished a house completely less than 100 yards away from us and killing everybody inside. Another V2 demolished a whole block of houses. A couple of miles away. We used to keep chickens for the eggs. I killed one once for us to have a meal. I had to strangle it, I don't want to do that again. My Mother used to feed them potato peelings. It seemed to work. We had fat hens and good eggs. Before the war I can remember the good meals we used to have. Steak and kidney pudding and steak and kidney pie, which I loved. Fried fish on Saturday which was kippers or herring. A meat joint on Sunday and we had to have cold meat on Monday Until chicken got popular and then we had the chicken on Sunday. Another day we would have steak and onions but it was only a cheap cut of steak. Sausage and mashed potatoes was good. It wasn't until I met Doreen, my second wife that I tasted Fillet Mignons for the first time. Her father was a butcher and I was 31 years old.

3A

We did eat pretty good although the cuts of meat and fish were the cheap cuts. I used to make toy lead soldiers from molds, just to make extra money. I also used to go chopping down trees for firewood. That would earn me about a dime, but it seemed a lot back then. When the war ended, I remember the big parties in the street. Everybody was happy, and all the wives were looking forward to the return of their husbands. I was very enterprising at a young age and always looking for ways to make money. I also did a paper round, not too keen on that. I had to get up too early in the morning. Then I did a bread and milk round. One woman gave me the equivalent of a quarter for a tip. I went back the following day to see if she had made a mistake. After all it was more than my days pay check. She said it was no mistake and that was my tip. The next job was the best. I got a job at a chemist shop. Doing odds and ends, filling empty bottles with shampoo and other stuff. Being amongst all the chemicals it made me want to play around with them at home, and do all kinds of experiments at home. I would do experiments with some of the acids, being very careful of course. I always made our vinegar at home. I stayed at that job until I left school at 14. I was 12 when I started my last job. At 12 years old the boys get together and start talking about girls and how they get pregnant and that their Peneus has other uses than to pee out of. Having sex at that age was unthinkable. Of course in the 21st century they even start younger than that. All I wanted to do was to kiss them. I was about 7 when I had my first kiss. She was a pretty little blonde and when I kissed her I noticed her nose was running. Put me right off, As she lived locally I watched her grow up and she married a black man and soon had a couple of kids. At 11 it was time to change schools. I went to Leggats Way, there

5

were 3 grades A.B.C. I managed to stay in the A. Grade while I was there I didn't make it to college. I don't think my parents realized how important it was. I certainly didn't.

My brother Chris was about 6 months old at this time. The best and highest paid job at this time was the printing trade. So that is what I wanted, But how to get it, that was the question. My Father had no connections with anybody, let alone the printing trade. I had an idea, I had been going to church, singing in the choir and all that good stuff. I talked to the Priest and asked him to get me into Odhams Watford. Now this place was the most fantastic place one would ever want to work. In the machine room it was filled with these German Goss Printing machines that went from floor to ceiling and they were printing magazines 3,000,000-4,000,000 run on each machine. These machines cost $2,000,000 each in the 1950s So when I got in I was overjoyed. I was only the general office boy, but then it was up to me. I needed a bike so my Father bought me one for a dollar. I needed it to run and get stamps, mail letters and get stuff for the office staff. My wage as an office boy was only $2 per week. It was a very interesting place to work. So many departments to check out on my rounds. There were 2 nice girls in the office, but at my age I was too scared to approach them. They were older than me anyway, but that doesn't stop you from wishing. After I had been there a year, I managed to talk myself into a job in the process department. I didn't think I was going to make it, as they said there were no vacancies but there was an opening in the foundry. This was good and the work was interesting, However at the last moment a vacancy was available in the process department, and I took it. This is where they prepared the cylinders for the big Goss printing machines. I got into the studio, which is what I wanted. I had always been interested in taking pictures with my 35mm and I was pretty good at it. We don't start our apprenticeship until we are 16 but they let us do certain jobs 'The wages were the pits, but after 5 years the money was the best in town. There was a girl in the neighborhood where I lived that used to hang around with us boys. Nice body and fair face. I knew she played around, I was too scared but I used my imagination.

4A

I joined the youth club at Callow land School. I was probably about 16 at this time. It was a good place to hang out and meet people. I used to go to Kingswood School also in the evenings. I got very competitive at table tennis and they always had leagues running on different nights of the week. I preferred Callow land. They seemed to have a bigger selection of girls. After 6 months they had the election of officers and I was elected chairman. I had to organize the dances, parties and what have you. It was the girls that elected me. When did I get so popular. I had so many girls available I didn't know what to do. I finished up doing nothing. I wasn't going to spoil my life getting a girl pregnant or catching V,D. Don't you wish you could go back sometimes. It was like having a gourmet buffet. r know how these rock stars feel. I had fun, getting the bands in, setting the prices and making sure everybody had a good time. At 16 you don't have too many women. You don't have to think about bills or food. I f you have your health you are lucky and enjoy yourself. I used to go dancing at Watford Town when they had their big dances. I met this girl, her name was Pam Wooster and she was a Coal Merchants daughter from Harrow Wealdstone. We were both 16 and I guess she was my first love although we didn't have sex or anything close. She was so pretty, she was just untouchable. I was just too young, I didn't know how to handle her. I had not acquired that something that I acquired later on in life. So nothing came of the romance I am sad to say. From 16- 18 I dated a few girls but nobody serious. I can't even remember their names. So I didn't have sex, that's for sure. I played a lot of tennis and table tennis during these years. I wish I had started at a young age. Would have been nice to play a sport you love and get paid for it. It was still good fun. Trouble was, all my girl friends were not the sporting kind and I didn't carry on with the tennis after I was 23. I was enjoying my job and I had managed to get into the color studio which was a lot more interesting than black and white. At 16 I had become an apprentice and by this time was using a motorized bike to get around. I did have a spell when I was 15 of touring round the countryside on my new bike which was a Hetchins. It was all chrome and had curly stays. I used to stay at Youth Hostels. It was fun at the time. I will never forget that bike. It was a racing bike and one day I did 120 miles in one day. I used to go with a friend from work as it could be lonely on your own. My Father was getting fed up painting houses and I managed to pull a few strings and get him a job where I worked. It was cleaning up sweeping up etc. It was more money than what he was getting and more benefit and with a Union and no more climbing ladders and he would be working inside. I leamt how to drive in my Fathers car and one day I would have one. I was 18 and waiting to get called up for National Service. I think I was almost 19 when I got them to report to Catterick Camp in Yorkshire. Can you imagine leaving home and going to an Army Barracks where you have to get up at 6am in the morning and get shouted at all day. This was a training camp and expect the worst. I suppose one could say that it was good for you. It makes a man out of you You have heard it all before. The training was interesting. I was trained as a wireless operator and a tank driver, both being rather fun. From what I can remember, the meals were not too bad. We had inspection by our beds every so often. I had forgotten to shine my boots this particular time, so I hid them. The officer said to me. Where are your boots? I said they are in for repair Sir. He checked up on me and found out I was lying. I got 7 days fatigues or extra duties is another name for it. Like peeling spuds and any other stuff they could throw at you. One soon got tired of the drill sergeant, but if you didn't do as he said he would take it out on you. We ran we marched with full packs. They were only trying to get us fit, after all. After 3-4 months I was I was assigned to the 9th Lancers stationed at Pencuik in Scotland near Edinburgh. Life was much better when you were in a regiment. It was a tank regiment but we were issued with long lances. Hence the name. We didn't have to get up so early and we got more leave. I would play cards most nights and would win at poker where I learnt how to play. After my initial training and before going to Scotland I managed to get a pass to go home. I had to hitch hike because I could not afford the train fare. It was a nice change to go home. The food was even better at the new camp. Most of the passes we had after that were not long enough to go home. From what I can remember it was almost 400 miles to home and I didn't have a car. I would go to Barrowland in Glasgow. That was a fun place to go dancing. I picked up a couple of girls on different visits. I was a pretty good dancer from 16 I did a lot of training with a Gold Medalist for ballroom dancing but there was no romance there. We continued our training on the tanks, how to advance without being noticed too much and more training on the radio.

5A

I went to the local dance and picked up this girl with the sole purpose of getting laid. She was not ugly, but you wouldn't want to take her home to Mom. She looked pretty good in the dark. I was 19 and it was time I got laid. There was snow on the ground and it was cold. I layed my army coat down on the ground in the snow. She laid on the coat, I pulled her skirt up and her pants down. I stripped to the waist and got on top. Of course I had to find out where to put it. I had seen pictures, she was pretty juicy and wanting it. We must have been locked together for at least 5 seconds, and that was it. I couldn't get out quick enough. I got too exited with no control. I didn't want to be giving her a baby. I felt so embarrassed I couldn't even enjoy my first sex act. I never made a date and I spent the next couple of months worrying if I had given her a baby or got infected with V.D. Next time I was luckier. I was at the same dance place and I spotted this beautiful blonde, very slim and standing against the wall. What you have to realize that this place was next to an Army camp and it was about 10 men to 1 woman. So I couldn't believe my luck when she let me walk her home. She soon became my regular girl friend. She was about 17 and it took me a few days before we had sex. I think she was a virgin because I couldn't find an opening anywhere. Looking back, it was probably my fault. Being too anxious and not getting the juices flowing. Once I did get going, at that age I could keep on going. And who knows about foreplay at that age. I was like a kid in a candy store. I had never known anything like it. I think I got every night off and I don't think there was restrictions regarding coming home at night. Her name was Betty and I saw her almost every night. We made love every time we met, I don't think we ever did anything else. I used a tablet that was supposed to kill the sperm. It seemed to work, or perhaps I was lucky. I had to go to summer camp for about a month, it was within 100 miles of our regular camp. It was for tank attack training and all I can remember was, we were always getting stuck in the mud and had to be winched out. Worst part being, I had to be away from my sex partner. Everything was the same when I got back. I had a spell when I had to do guard duty on Edinburgh Castle. We were guarding the Crown Jewels and had real revolvers and they were loaded. I think we did 2 hours on and 4 off through the night. Makes me tired thinking-about it. I also did guard duty at Holly Rood Palace and was inspected by the Queen Mother and Princess Margaret They actually spoke to me and shook my hand. I still have the photographs. All good things come to an end and it was the end of my Army Service. So it was goodbye Betty, My girl friend and back home we go. We did keep in touch and we arranged to meet at Margate on the S.E Coast of England, which was a seaside resort. We met and everything was fine. We went swimming, we walked along the seafront and did everything one does on vacation. Towards the end of the vacation I found myself getting tired of my Army romance. I told her that everything was over. I don't know why, because I had no replacement in Watford. I guess I thought that she lived too far away to carry on a romance, and I knew that I wouldn't be getting married to this girl. I suppose I had screwed her so many times that I was ready for something new. I was only a novice in the art of making love anyway. So it is back to the youth clubs again and I am also back at Odhams. They cut in half the time spent in the Forces, so my new total time would be 4 years 2 months, less time already served. Getting back to the Youth Clubs. I met Nadine at Kingswood Youth Club, who I would eventually get married to. She was always hanging around with her friend Sheila. Nadine was a beautiful girl with a nice figure and nice to look at and big breasts. I soon struck up a relationship with her. It wasn't based on sex. In fact I can't remember us having sex for quite a while after our first meeting. There was a tragedy in her family. Her brother who was about 5 years older, died in a local train crash. I think he had just got married or was very close to it. Nadine and I were going together for about 3 years. I really loved this girl and it was lovey dovey all through our courtship for about 3 years and then we got married. All our friends were getting married, so you have to follow the flock. I was 23 and had finished my apprentichip and was getting good money. What do you know about love at that age. I loved this girl and was sure it was for life. We rented a place for 6 weeks and then bought a house in Coates Way Garston. It was brand new and cost about $4,000. When we had settled in I became a little restless and wanted to do something in addition to my job. There was this block of shops with accommodation over. We sold the house and I put in television sets and small appliances and later put in wool and all sorts of stuff. Nadine's mother would run the shop during the day and I would install the T.V.s When I came home from work. We had to put a store front in, but I watched carefully so that I could do the next one. I kept the store about 2 years and then sold it and made $8,000 profit. I bought a brand new Sunbeam Rapier. Yvon had been born while we had the T.V. store. Now I was looking to go into something else.

6A

First of all I had to get a new house. We found one in Chesham, which was not too far away from the next venture. The house was nice and being new, all we had to do was move in the furniture. I can't remember what our furniture was like, but I am sure it was nice. The next store was in Chorleywood. It was a country town. Not to far from the big towns with the big stores. Middle to upper class people and some nice properties. I thought they needed a hardware store, selling pots and pans, tools, screws, and gift items. I saved on the shop front this time. I had found out where to buy all the materials and I got a handyman to put it together. I could have done it myself but I have to see about ordering the inventory and all that good stuff. During this time, Linda was born. I had witnessed Yvon being born before, but I didn't need to see a repeat with Linda. I was still working at Odhams, so I had to cover with part time staff when I was at work. During this time Nadine and her sister Meryl went away to Ramsgate or Margate, (They are right next to one another, I can never remember) with all the kids and stayed in a caravan/trailer for a week. As fate would have it I used to pass this sexy blond every morning on the way to work. I had upgraded from the old $90 van to a new van for the new business. She gave me that come and get me smile, so I stopped and asked her if she would like a lift. I dropped her off and made a date with her. As Nadine was away, I saw her every night that first week. I was 29 and she was in her teens. We went through a lot of heavy petting, but she wouldn't go all the way. If she can withstand my gentle persuasion for so long, she must be a virgin. Then Nadine was back, I wasn't going to let all that preparation work go to waste, so I had to make excuses to go out 3 times a week. Marion had to be in by 10pm so that wasn't too hard.

I had foam squares and a blanket in the back of the van. After the first week we would go to a remote place and she was ready. She must have been dreaming about sex. Thats all she wanted every night and she loved it. One week I took Yvon for a holiday at Butlins Holiday Camp. It was just the two of us. It was about 100 miles away. I said to Marion, if you want to come down on the train and ride back with us, it would be nice. Yvon and I had a nice time. Butlins are great Camps They had this beauty contest. I was chatting to one of the winners. I can't even remember her name. I didn't get her phone number either, I must be slipping. She was from Birmingham 5 foot 9 ins, brunette 115 Ibs and beautiful with a gorgeous figure. Before I knew it, I was in bed with her having a great time. A pity I never met her on the first night. I would have been making trips to Birmingham. They had a child sitting service, so I knew Yvon would be okay. We met Marion outside the camp gates. She was there when we left the campground. I rigged up some type of curtain in the back of the van. We stopped in a secluded area on the way home. I told Yvon that we were all going to have a little sleep. She was to stay in the front and I was going to get in the back with Aunty. I had continuous sex for about 3 hours (I could at that age). Yvon still remembers the aunt and Yvon is 52 now. All good things come to an end, Nadine thought I was playing table tennis on my nights away. But one night she opens the glove compartment and sees lipstick tissues. I had no excuse, that is what you get when you screw teenagers. I had to confess, so I had to cease operations. I hate to say this, but Marion was so sexy I knew I was going to miss her. If she had been older I might have left home just for the sex. I couldn't get the same satisfaction from Nadine. Looking back, I blame myself for not being more patient with her. Sex doesn't always come natural to every woman. I sold the hard ware store in less than a year and did pretty well. By this time I was thinking I could run any business, So my next business was to be a ladies beauty shop.

7A

The site was Rickmansworth on a main road in the center of town. It was not my intention to work in the shop, but I wanted to know all about Ladies Hairdressers so that I could converse and give opinions with the best of them. While the lease was being prepared and I was fitting out the shop, I took a course in London at one of the best schools. While in London I would go for judo lessons in the evenings. I was taught by a 6th. Dan black belt, who was probably one of the best in the world. I also joined a local club. It was a good confidence builder. Judo taught you how to fall and through the years I am sure it has helped me relax and save me from hurting myself. During the early stages I did dislocate my elbow, but that was soon fixed at the Hospital. I got a manager for the beauty shop, but I still had to be there for the start up. I had to leave the printing trade temporarily. I had clients asking for me to do their hair, so what could I do, I had to oblige. It didn't take me long to realize that I could make more money back at the printing company. I got a job at Sun Printers. They did the same sort of work as Odhams and I needed a change anyway. I did spend time in the shop also. Roy who was the manager, was pretty good, but not really up with some of the modern trend. Then there was Doreen. She worked at another beauty shop 50yds down the road. She came in to see me and said that she would like to come and work at our shop. She said she was not happy at the other shop. I took her on of course. I had been admiring this beauty walk by my shop every day for the past month. She was sexy with a trim figure and also had a pretty face, and was single as I learnt later. She was a fantastic Hairdresser and could work at about 3 times as fast as anybody else. I was in her pants in no time. She was hot and it was good sex. When all the staff had gone we would go to the back of the shop and make love for hours. I had to replace Marion after all. Doreen was more mature, she was 21 and I was 31 and she had been married before and she had a little boy of 5 who was being brought up by her in-laws. Doreen lived with her father and his second wife. Doreen had two younger sisters. I did get to meet them all including Paul her son. I think I was hypnotized by Doreen. I decided to leave Nadine and the children, which was a horrible and stupid thing to do. I can't believe that I left this beautiful woman and my children, who had done nothing wrong. For a new piece of arse. It wasn't as if I was in love. It was just sex. I will never forget the day I told Nadine the news. It must have been hard for her to bring up the kids on her own. I feel guilty about everything I done, but one can't turn back the clock. I wish she had got married again, I know she had chances. I just want to say how sorry I am. Nadine was everything a man could wish for. I could have taught her a few things sexually. I was just rotten to the core. Doreen and I rented a place with Stuart our accountant. He was gay, but a nice guy. In the early days of parting I would visit the kids, but Doreen used to get into such a jealous mood that I had to give it up. I bought a house at Croxley Green near Watford. Doreen was still working at the beauty shop and the house was close by. It was a nice house with a nice garden, but it wasn't new. I was still at the Sun Printers which was also close by. I put the beauty shop up for sale. I don't keep anything long, I just like to turn a quick profit and then on to the next venture. We went to visit Doreen's Mother somewhere in Kent, she was strange, but it takes all sorts to make the world go round. Thinking back about Nadine, She was well rid of me. During one of our arguments or misunderstandings. I can't remember what caused it. I cleared off to Paris by car which was about 275 miles. I had no girlfriend with me so it was before Doreen came along. Had a great time visiting all the sights and night life. It was my first visit to Paris. How mean can you get, that was one of the most selfish acts I have ever performed. Why didn't I take the family? Having sold the beauty shop I was looking for another business. I had this Post Office at Chorleywood in mind. I knew the area and this time it was a going business with a rent with option to purchase. I knew I could make money on a resale. It had living accommodation above the shop so I sold our house and moved in. Everyone goes to the Post Office, and we sold candy, greeting cards and gifts and all sorts. Plus we got paid by the Postmaster for selling stamps and stuff. The accommodation was good. Clive was actually born here.

It wasn't planned. I am sure Doreen planned it so that we would have to get married. We did get married

1 month before Clive was born. No big wedding as Doreen was 8 months pregnant. Just a few relations and friends. I think the first vacation Doreen and I had was when we had sold the beauty shop. It was Christmas time and we went to Butlins Holiday Camp. We traveled in thick snow there and back, We had a good time, but I don't think it is the place to take a woman. Some may not understand, but it is like taking coals to Newcastle. I won the competition for being the best groomed man.

8A

Our next vacation started off in Malaga, Spain. We didn't take Clive as he was only 6 weeks old. It was probably her Dad's wife Doris who looked after him. We had fun on the beach and the night life was good. Then we decided to visit Morocco and saw Tangiers and Casablanca. Some of these places can be very dangerous at night. There were beggars in the street, some of which I am told, cut off their limbs so they can beg for money. I bought some nice leather goods in Casa Blanca. I still have a full length leather coat that is like brand new. We went on a few vacations. Mainly to different parts of Spain and Majorca and to Rimini on the Adriatic coast of Italy. Clive was with us but he probably won't remember. It was time to sell the Post Office. It was an easy sell. Someone close to London bought it. They wanted to buy the business and the property I borrowed a small amount of money from my Father for me to buyout the option first. I wouldn't need the money for long. After doing me that small favor I bought him a brand new car. A printing company in Liverpool called Bembrose was offering good money for the guys at Watford to come and work. I thought it would be a nice change so Doreen stayed with her family until I could fix up a house. Fixing up the job was no problem and it was a nice place to work and more money. I rented a place in Liverpool, but not fit enough for the family. I bought a brand new house in Formby. and in less than 6 weeks from my leaving home, we were all settled in. After having the baby, Doreen was off sex for a while. I don't think she ever got back to what she was when we first met. I do know that it changes a woman sometimes when they have babies. I had an Aunt Leyla that lived in Lytham St Annes which was about 50 miles from our house. She was married to Bill but married late at 41 for the first time. She was my

Mother's older sister, she was pretty too. She stayed at home looking after her mother and never going out. Bill was a nice guy, no oil painting, but they seemed happy. Doreen took a liking to Leyla and we saw them often. Among other things Leyla taught her to crochet. Doreen had a lot of good qualities. She kept a good house and she was always clean and tidy and she didn't waste money.

We liked it up here so it was time to get another business going. I looked around for another store to rent. I found one and decided to open another hardware store in Gateacre near Liverpool. My Mother never liked Doreen and though my Father never said I don't think he liked her either. Anyway I filled the store with all the usual stuff plus a lot of gift items and the shop took off well. Doreen was running it and I was working at Bembrose. All she had to do was take the money, everything was there ready. After a while I put an add in to sell the shop. I got an enquiry from Harvey Guratsky. He was a Jew but he was okay. He wanted to go into partnership with me and open a small chain of Hardware and Gift stores. I knew he would be picking my brains. Doreen took an instant dislike to him. From what I can remember she seemed jealous of the time Harvey and I spent together. We bought 2 new vehicles and 2 trailers and we would go to Manchester where all the inexpensive gifts were and fill our vehicles and trailers up to the top. By this time I had left the printing firm, never to return. It is always best to be your own boss. Doreen and I had another vacation at another holiday camp. It was a bit more classy than Butlins. The rooms were better, it was just better all round. Doreen had a miscarriage, this again was an unplanned thing by both of us. She was learning how to water ski and the pull of the boat with a jerking action did the trick. It was a blessing in disguise as Clive was only about a year old. She had to spend a few hours in Hospital.

9A

We had 4 stores and a distribution center within 3 years and doing pretty
well. I had left the Printing Company as I was the brains of the organization
I was needed. Harvey had got a divorce since starting the new venture
and I think he was taking out Nina the manager of the Kirkby store, but
I didn't ask questions. He was learning the business fast and so was Nina.
I was knocking off Pauline who was the cashier. I don't know where we
got her from, but she should have been a model. Beautiful face and perfect
figure. Long blonde hair. It only happened a couple of times. I didn't
think it was a good idea to play around with the staff. She was so nice and
if I had been working at that branch, it would have been a regular thing I
am sure. That was the first time I had been unfaithful to Doreen, She never
found out anyway and she wasn't being all that friendly to me. Pauline
was about 22 and single with no baggage. Doreen didn't get on well
with Nina,but Harvey and I got on well together. We had settled Clive
in a Jewish school close by. We also moved to Kirkby from the Formby
house. At this moment I can't think why. It was more central to the stores.
Doreen was getting bored with being at home all day. Looking back I
think she would have been happier getting a job in the beauty business.
I don't know what happened with her. I know she didn't like Nina and
in fact she was making too many decisions was getting on her nerves. I
got home from work one night and she was packed and ready to go. She
didn't say where she was going and I didn't ask, She took Clive with her.
To this day I do not know what caused the break up. That is what I saw it
as, and to this day, I don't know what caused the separation. Harvey and
his friend Nina decided that they wanted to buy me out. If I had been in
Real Estate and know what I know now, he wouldn't have bought me out

so cheap. Okay I have this pocket full of money, so to speak and what do I do next. I buy a Greek Restaurant, fully staffed, thank the lord. I know zip about the business. What counts is managing people and I can do that. I had the job of taking the orders and seating people, banking the money, and that was about it to start. The head waiter took care of ordering the wines and the food. I am glad that Doreen cleared off when she did. Now I don't have to include her in my plans for the restaurant. Having a kid with her, she must have gone to her Mums or Dads house, take a guess. I don't care anymore. She probably wanted time on her own, but that is not the way to do it. I know she didn't find out about Pauline because that was kept very secret. While I was waiting for the restaurant deal to go through, a friend of mine from Chorleywood who used to come into my hardware store to buy stuff, asked me if I would like to fit out a store, inside and store front in stainless steel. It was the wife that wanted this shop and it was 200 miles away in London. I bet they are not together now. She had a roving eye and not only that, she was always full of life. She said price was no object. Meanwhile I went to a dance in Liverpool and picked up this cute little blonde. She was about 17 but she was well shaped and would keep me warm for a couple of weeks. I took her out a couple of times to make sure she performed to my satisfaction, She was great and also wanted to come away with me. She was a pretty blonde and I met with the family and the family had no objections. Can you beat that. I took a couple of workmen with me, and I had to have all the materials ready and keep my eye on them. In the end they let me down. They said they were homesick and had to go home. I had to chase around for a handyman to finish the job, which was a pain in the arse. Everything turned out good and I had a nice 2 weeks making love to somebody fresh, I didn't keep her for too long, at that age they are only good for one thing. So I am still in the Kirkby house and Doreen shows up one day, It doesn't take her long to spot all the long blonde hairs in the bed. She goes crazy, picks up a carving knife and chases me round the room. I was quick in those days, I just dodged the knife and took it off her. I said I haven't heard from you for a month, what do you expect me to do Sit around and mope.

10A

I never did go back in the Print again, but my brother Chris started work at Odhams in the planning department and my Father worked there until he retired. Now I was looking forward to making something of this restaurant called La Tava. Doreen says, you can take Clive. He was only 7 years old. Then walked out. Now I had to get rid of the house at Kirkby because the restaurant had a little house that was included in the sale. It was going to take me a couple of months to get organized with the restaurant and I had to wait at least a month before the loan was in place. I had to get some friends to look after Clive. I can't remember how long but it wasn't long. Clive is always moaning about it even today. I should have dumped him when his Mother did. I settled into a nice apartment one block from the beach at Southport until the restaurant was ready. All I needed now was a beautiful girl to keep me company. Doreen had gone, for the time being anyway. Thinking back now, I should have gone after Pauline from Kirkby. She was tried and tested and she was gorgeous, I don't know where my brain was back then. So it is back to the dance at Liverpool, Where I pick up all my spares. This time her name was Joy and she really was a bundle of Joy. She was ready for sex any place anytime. All my girls, even one night stands are within certain weight limits and are nice to look at. So that I don't have to mention it every time. Joy lived at home with Mum and Dad. She was about 19. I never got to meet her family. A friend of mine told me that she had a black Father and that is why I never got to meet the family. No one would ever guess, she was looking pretty white to me and I wasn't looking for a bride anyway. She was a brunette and looked and talked as if she was educated. Before Doreen and I separated I bought this old wooden boat intending to use it for skiing. We took it to the ocean once to learn to ski. Just ordinary skiing is pretty easy when you got the hang of it. Another thing that I had forgotten. Doreen and I went to a holiday camp when Clive was a year old. It was an upscale camp. Much better than Butlins with much better accommodation. We were taking turns to be pulled off the jetty by a speedboat. We were on water skis. It was the pull of the rope from the boat. The jerking motion gave her a miscarriage. She stayed overnight at the local Hospital. This was a blessing in disguise. We did go to Butlins the first Christmas we were together. I remember driving in thick snow it must have been at least 100 miles each way. I got first prize for hest groomed man. There is always something to do and from what I remember the food was okay. Reminds me of the time I was 16 and 6 of us rented a car and drove to one of the Butlins 200 miles away. We took it in turns to drive, it is a wonder we made it with all the change of drivers. I can even remember drinking whisky to get drunk to give me courage to pick up a girl. None of us were lucky, but we had a great time and there were loads of things to do and competitions to enter. We all wished we were Redcoats. The girls would flock around them, even the ugly ones. Surprising what a uniform does for you. They were the ones that organized the entertainment. I think we would have done their job for nothing. It was about a month that I stayed in the apartment in Southport. Joy stayed most nights and then I moved into the little house next to the restaurant which wasn't too great. There was a lot of mildew but I knew that I would rebuild as soon as I had got things organized. The main thing was to get ready for Christmas and I took over on Nov. 22nd 1972 which doesn't give me a lot of time. I think I will keep Joy for a while. I had a good Head Waiter and his wife Mercedes was the hest chef in the world, in my opinion.

11A

All the staff were Spanish except one and he was Portugese Ramond, one of the Spanish waiter used to sing along with the band when he wasn't busy. Mercedes had a sister who was also a good chef and her husband was a waiter. They all lived above the restaurant and their kids. It must have been pretty cramped. I can't ever remember checking the place out They never complained and they were not getting charged for accommodation. I was with all these guys for 9 years and nobody ever left me. Of course we did add to the staff as we got bigger. They all spoke Spanish and I didn't understand them. I am sure they were cussing me out sometimes. Most of the time we all got on well together. I should have learnt the language but I was lazy. They all spoke fluent English so why bother. Salvador the head waiter was fantastic. He could do anything, and he was handsome too. The filet mignons dishes, Steak Diane and all the other dishes he would cook at the table. Looked very impressive. All the servings to our customers were silver service. We had a band Tuesday, Friday and Saturday and people would come 40 miles to eat and dance at La Tava. The food was so good. I would do a Dinner Dance menu on a Saturday with a choice of about 8 entrees various starters and deserts for a set price. Sirloin Steak was on the menu, but as it was a Greek Restaurant, most people wanted to try our Greek dishes. Which we could make a lot cheaper. At the end of the day , all the staff got fed and Saturday lunch time the regulars got Sirloin Steak. All things had been set up before I took over, which was good, it is a lot easier taking over a running business than having to start from scratch. (Been there, done that) Now Christmas is here and I am in a pickle. People are coming from everywhere and trying to get a table. I don't like turning them away, but I should have done. Some had been waiting an hour for a table, and not enough room to sit down in the lounge to have your drink. I could seat about 100 in the dining area, but only about 30 in the lounge. I will change all that as soon as possible. Did you ever hear that story about every one getting sick on the plane including the pilots. So sick that everyone was passing out except one person who was a pilot. That story motivated me to get my license. I took lessons at Woodvale nr. Southport. And got my pilots license. I told her about that story. She said, if you are a pilot, the principles are the same with all airplanes. In other words, you would be able to fly the plane. There was a big lake, not too fur away with a lot of boats whizzing around. The name was Carr Mill. I dragged my old wooden boat up there. I decided I had to upgrade because this club was a racing club. I bought a fibre glass v hull boat and named it Arctic Fox. It had a maximum speed of 45 mph and it would still be okay for skiing. The races were handicap so that everyone stood a chance. I won a lot of cups with this boat, but clearly I had bought the wrong boat I wanted to go fast and 45 mph was not fast. I eventually swopped it for a real racing boat that would do 100 mph. Then I graduated from National to International rating on my license and I only raced on lakes, Lake Windermere being one of them. I could never win against these world class guys. I knew I was as good as them, but I couldn't afford to buy all the latest refinements and new engines that these guys were getting, They were backed by the makers of the engines. I only had one flip on my boat. There was a lot of activity and the water was rough with all the boats charging round. My left sponson dug in on a corner and flipped me out of the boat. I was lucky, the boat did a complete somersault and landed the correct way up. My only concern was getting chopped up by the propellers, but they do slow down when there is a man in the water. We wore orange overhauls so that we would be spotted. I used to wear a suit underneath. They called me the James Bond of racing.

12A

Joy always came to the races with me. Clive would also come and watch me race. I had a friend that I used to race with, his name was Jeff Lightfoot We had some good times together. I wonder what happened to him, he was a little older than me. Pretty handsome guy and liked the women. He was in construction. I had to get in 40 hours before I could take my pilots license test One of my tests was to fly to an airport in the middle of nowhere and land and get a signature and return to home base. I had a problem flying the plane and trying to read the map. I am afraid I got lost, we couldn't use the V.O.R position finder. I was lost with a quarter tank of gas, I wasn't scared, I could put this sucker down anywhere. I called my instructor for instructions. She was a woman and I am sure she passed out. She said that I was to land at Liverpool Airport and declare an emergency. Can you imagine all the fire engines chasing around. As for finding the airport, a blind man could find it. She met me there and thinking I was scared and nervous, flew me back to Woodvale. I felt fine but she felt better flying me. After all I hadn't got my license yet. I did do a perfect landing, so I must have felt okay. There was another incident, I had my license this time. I flew to an airport about one and a half hours away. It was easy to find, I just had to track along the coast. I did have a woman with me, but I can't remember who. We landed safely and had a snack. Then I suddenly realized we had one and a half hours flying time and if we left right away, it would still be dark when we got to Woodvale. We took off and I had it on full throttle all the way. It was dark and when I landed but I had a couple of lessons landing in the dark, so they came in handy. Nobody said anything so it was okay. If I had been a cautious person I would have returned in the morning. I started planning the

restaurant extension, but before I could do anything I had to make a deal with the farmer. We came to an agreement, so that was great. It would give me more room for parking, lounge extension and a new house. I Got all the work done by individual tradesmen and built a super big house. All under my supervision of course. I was so proud of what I did. You wouldn't have recognized the place. We could seat about 150 in the lounge area now. I put in another bar and spruced up the kitchen. I remember digging the footings for the house. There was one section I couldn't find a solid bottom. I must have gone down about 8 foot and I got them to keep pouring the concrete before the sides caved in. I expected to get a crack on that side of the house, but even when I checked it out 1997 , about 20 years later, there were no cracks in the walls. So I did a good job building that place. I never closed the restaurant while I was doing the alterations. We are getting ahead of ourselves here. We are in 1973 and it was in the middle of 1976 when we started the alterations. I just had to manage with the badly designed place for about another 3 years. I wanted to put Clive into a private school just down the road, which would have been good for him. He wouldn't go so he went to the local school 200 yards from the restaurant. Remembering last Christmas and the mess I was in. I decided to print tickets for the holiday period. We had a lot of parties booking in large numbers. Lets say we had a booking for 20 people and only 16 showed up. That would have been a loss to us of say $100. With my system it would be their loss. Usually when a person has paid in advance, they always seem to show up. I don't know where I get these ideas from as I don't know of anyone else that was doing the same thing. We always provided a live band, and they were very good and we had a small dancing area for our customers.We had the band Tuesday, Friday, and Saturday all year round. Tuesday night was quiet, so I came up with another idea. I called it a party night, I had tickets printed saying that the main course was free, and I gave these tickets out to all the customers that came in on the other nights to encourage them to come in on a Tuesday. Bad idea giving food away, I don't think so. People drank, and also they had starters and deserts, not all of them, but it takes a crowd to create an atmosphere. I kept all these ideas going while I owned La Tava.

13A

It was about this time in early 1974 when the pretty girl from the advertising company called to see me about advertising in the local newspaper. I go into more detail in my notes later. Everything is going fine and I think I know how to run a restaurant. No problems with the staff and they all seem to get on well together. Sometimes I go over to the restaurant in the morning to have coffee and toast. I am living on my own with Clive, and I know I could have any meal I wanted from the restaurant, but I would rather make something just for Clive and I. How crazy is that. Our favorite for breakfast was bacon and tomatoes and we liked the tomatoes burnt. I still see Joy almost every night to satisfy my sexual appetite. We sometimes go over to the restaurant and have a drink and a meal. Makes a change from having sex all the time. Clive is a heavy sleeper so we don't disturb him. It is the middle of 1974 and I am thinking it is time I had somebody new besides Joy. So I am off to Liverpool to see what new talent is floating around. I am having a good time at the dance. I am standing around, watching what is going on. I do quite a bit of dancing and am not the shy type that is afraid to ask a girl to dance. I don't have to be smoking to calm my nerves. Anyway, I saw this blonde girl fall down a couple of stairs. She looked about 30 which was a bit old from my usual, but will be okay for a spare as I only have Joy and I like a reserve in case one takes a hike. I helped her up and started chatting to her. She was very sexy, but she was married and she had 3 kids. Too much baggage and not for me, but she had a nice trim figure and I was definitely going to sample it. What was she doing on her own at a dance, she must have wanted sex

on the side. She was good at sex and had no trouble giving me everything on the first date. She knew how to open her legs and move just right and she loved it and couldn't get enough of me. Her name was Brenda and she had 3 boys, Paul who was the same age as Clive, Graham the middle one who I didn't get to know and Kerry the oldest, eventually worked as a waiter under Salvador. I never had any communication with her husband, He must have been glad to get rid of her. I eventually moved Brenda and Paul in with us. I don't know why, it was a crazy move because when Joy found out, she said you can't have me and this other woman, so she left me, never to be seen again. I decided that we would take a family vacation to Paris. Brenda and Paul and Clive and I. We would hire a caravan and tow it with the car that I had. So off we go leaving Salvador to run the place. I am speeding down the motorway on the way to Dover and Brenda says, can I drive for a while. She is driving for 5 minutes and she jacknifes the whole unit. She could have killed us all. She damaged the caravan and busted a wheel. We were stranded for 6 hours but we still made Paris. We went everywhere and saw the sights, but I don't think Paris was the ideal choice when you have kids with you. We stayed in camps that had all the facilities. But sometimes the kids were a pain in the but. When we got home, the house next door had almost burnt down and we were lucky La Tava was still standing. A workman was using a blow torch to remove paint from the eaves and had accidently caught the roof on fire and the house was severely damaged. Brenda had a job so she was out of my hair during the day. Another year goes by and Brenda is still around. She must be good in bed or doing something right. I can't remember which. We decided to go on a skiing vacation I had never had that kind of holiday before so I thought it would be nice. I thought Austria would be a nice location. We got a nice place with loads of snow and high mountains. First of all they had to teach us how to ski safely. So we start on the small slopes and learn how to stop and turn. After about 3 days I was skiing from over 5,000 feet mountains and managing to stay up on two feet. I loved it, I can't believe I never went back. The evening entertainment was good. Everybody was so friendly and there was lots to do. We are up to the beginning of 1976 and I am expanding with something different. I am buying a roadhouse for truck drivers. To eat and for sleeping I am calling it the Silent Seventh. Brenda has been looking for something to do and she wants to run it. I can't remember what happened to Paul. It was the long summer of 1976 and so hot and no rain. Two young couples came into the restaurant laughing and joking and having a good time. Both the women were nice. I took a fancy to the brunette and something clicked between us. I made a date with Val for the next day at lunch time. I played all my moves when I met her but couldn't get her into bed.

14A

We met the following day and the day after. By this time I must have slept with her. I would say to her Fillet Mignons is nice, but regard me as Lobster. I am just a change in the menu. We would meet about 11 am and she would go at 3 pm 5 days per week for nearly 5 years. We would have sex every time we met, that would be over 1,000 times if anyone is counting. She was always so fresh and clean. Not a hair out of place. Dressed to kill with her high heel shoes. For it to last as long as it did, I think we had something more than sex. I was getting the best of her every time. I didn't see when she first got out of bed or when she was in her scruffy clothes. She had a little boy who I never met. That is why she always had to leave at 3 pm to pick him up from school. She was quite happy staying married so I had the best of both worlds. Sometimes we would eat at my Restaurant. Salvador got to know her pretty well. Other times we would take a ride out in the country and have lunch and then go back for the loving. Her husband never found out and he was a real nice guy. Perhaps I was doing him a favor, stopping her from going elsewhere. They would come in the restaurant on a Saturday night and I would sit at their table to say hello and Valerie would play Footsie with me under the table. I think we only went out 2 times in the evening and I went to her house only once. One of the times I went out in the evening I got food poisoning and she had to drive me home I will never forget that summer of 1976 with sunshine every day for at least 6 weeks. We both loved Johnny Mathis and the record, when will I see you again by the Supremes. She knew I was going out with Brenda, But she accepted it, but probably didn't like it when you think about it Val had a lot more sex from me than her husband. I had a friend called Jimmy. I didn't see him often and he was always into something. He had this gorgeous brunette as a girlfriend, She was about 20 and he was in his forties and they had invited us to dinner. Not only was this girl a peach, she was very clever. Jimmy was no oil painting so I don't know how they connected. They were living together, I wonder where they are now. This is what he said to me. Ken, why don't you get a younger model. What a cheek that man has, but I did agree with him. Brenda was too old for me. I thought at the time, I wouldn't mind taking your girlfriend off your hands, but restrained myself. But you do not steal from your buddies do you? I haven't mentioned cars, but I have always had a nice car. Soon after buying La Tava I bought an Audi with only 5 cylinders but that car would get up and go and I really enjoyed it. Then I bought a new Triumph P.I. because my friend Jeff Lightfoot had one and I liked the performance. I can't remember how long I had it, but there was this guy in the Isle of Man had bought this 12 cylinder Jaguar open top sports car. He was over 70 years old and he was scared of the car. I said what about an exchange with say $2,000 and a Triumph P.I. I went over right away before he could change his mind. The car was brand new with not more than 500 miles on the clock. We did the deal with both parties happy. The restaurant was doing fabulous, it sure was a good buy and has given me a lot of happy times. Monday we were closed, Tuesday, Friday and Saturday are now good Thursday is quiet, but that is okay, but I have to do something with Sunday. I did something which wouldn't have worked in America It was a turkey Sunday Lunch Carvery, serving turkey and vegetables and all the trimmings with a simple desert for a fixed price, eat as much as you want. I had a chef in uniform, carving the 40 pound turkey, Serving lunch only until they stopped coming. They were lining up to eat. It did so well I put it on for Thursday Evening our quiet night. It was 1977 and the improvements were finished and I had a big beautiful house to live in and a fantastic remodeled restaurant. I saved such a lot of money on different things. I bought 150 chairs and I had to put them all together to save money. That was for the new lounge. It broke my heart when I visited the old place in 1997 on vacation from America La Tava had closed down because I am sure of bad management. When I left in 1981 the place was hopping and I had every day covered. He even screwed me out of $80,000 on the note before he went bust. Salvador gave Clive a job as a waiter and he met a few nice girls and it helped to get him started. One of the girls he met was invited to our home in America, that would be in 1982 and she stayed for 2 weeks and had a good time, but they never kept in contact. It is just too far away to carry on a romance. The night I met

Diane was on Saturday. I saw this brunette dancing. Good looking, super figure and about 25 years old. I have found my replacement for Brenda. This is the younger model I have been looking for. She has a daughter of about seven from a previous marriage. She was gorgeous too. I took her home that night, she had her own house so that was nice, It was the ideal situation to make my first move. I was 48 and past my prime ,so I thought. We had a great night, I think I climaxed 17 times. And kept going for at least 2 hours. If anyone had told me that story I wouldn't have believed them. As one gets older, one can only dream about things like that. I am sure she would confirm if she is single.

15A

And if you are still having sex at 75 it is probably only once each time. Diane and I had some nice vacations. The first one was to Butlins so that we could take the kids. Butlins is always good and everyone had a good time. Then we had a couple of 7 day cruises. Her brother Brian and his wife came with us on one of the cruises. She was an eye catcher, but I had to keep my eyes off her, otherwise I think I would have been in big trouble. The ship that Diane and I was on by ourselves was a Christmas cruise and they served us hamburgers for Christmas dinner, and the food was not up to standard. Shows and entertainment were great, and there was always something to do on board ship. It was a rocky rolling ride at times, because the seas were rough. The best cruise by far was on the Oriana, we had a 3 week trip to the Caribbean and back. It was great with so much to do. They were teaching us to make all sorts of things while we were at sea. On board was the world champion bridge player. He was Russian and he was giving classes to anybody that wanted to learn. Me being a games player, got in on the act. My brother Chris who I don't see very often, teaches bridge now that he has retired. I have only seen him about 4 times in the last 50 years and about the same for phone calls. He has his own web site for bridge information. We visited a lot of ports, it is always fun checking out the local arts and crafts on the different Islands and having fun on the beautiful beaches. I can't remember all the places we visited. I personally have been on more than 30 cruises and most of them were in the Caribbean and the cruise with Diane was over 30 years ago. One place we stopped at was Dominique. A very small Island with very little to do and see. I was on my way back to the ship and this native of the Island wanted me to buy his boat. It was about 3 foot by 3 foot and made out of bamboo and it had sails on it and looked very nice. I didn't pay much because I am a wheeler dealer anyway. I got it on board ship and put it over my bed in the cabin, I woke up in the middle of the night and there were soldier ants crawling all over me, Scared the shit out of me, they were big suckers, but they must have liked me because they didn't bite me. I was as mad as hell. I called the cabin Stewart and ask for a quick cabin change because we were getting eaten alive by these big ants. In the new cabin we had the same trouble. You guessed it they were coming from the ship that I had bought. I wonder if Diane remembers about the bamboo ship. It is sitting in front of me right now. First thing I did was to debug the ship. They came crawling out to die by the hundred. That ship has traveled 1,000s of miles. Looking a bit rough, I will have to give it a makeover. For birth protection Diane was not too happy with the pill, so she got a plastic ring fitted to her uterus to prevent getting pregnant. I must have been with this girl for at least 4 years and eventually I got the vasectomy, good choice for now, but not for when I went to America and met Teresa. I have been very lucky I haven't put anybody in the family way. Before the pill I just used an oversized pill that was supposed to kill the sperm. I would never use a condom, I like to feel the flesh. Now with aids it is a different story and I am glad I am not playing the field any more. When I think of it, the chances the girls take, They deserve a medal. I must have been with Brenda about 4 years too. I told her that I was replacing her but she could have Silent Seventh if she wanted it. I didn't own the place, it was a lease. We were still on good terms. I went by a couple of times to service her. Then I thought about all these horny truck drivers chatting her up and remembering how sexy she is. I might pick up something and pass on to my Ormskirk lady which I would feel real bad about. Valerie did not like it at all when I got rid of Brenda for Diane. I said, what difference does it make, we are still in the same situation. You have me in the daytime and she has me at night, but you are number one. However when I knew I was leaving, we drifted apart, it was a mutual thing, but I don't know what really happened, but I suppose, nothing lasts forever.

16A

Diane and I took a trip to New York in 1979. After flying to New York and seeing all the sights. Empire State Building, Statue of Liberty and all the other good stuff. We boarded a Greyhound bus and off to Miami we go. We stayed at a hotel on the beach and for our first look at Florida it seemed pretty good. While staying at the hotel I got a message to say my Mother had died of double pneumonia at the age of 71. She was at that time paralyze and it had got worse over the years, and it started in her little finger and went right through her body. My Father had died 3 years earlier at 68 of cancer of the bowels. I couldn't do much 4,000 miles away and they were going to hold the funeral until we got back. On the way back we stopped at the Capital and saw all the sights. Capital building and the museum and other good stuff and finally New York. I hate bus trips, but how else are you going to see all these places. Before selling La Tava I bought another really big restaurant called The Hayfield, situated on a busy road in Ormskirk. It was on 2 floors, downstairs was operating as a la carte and upstairs was empty. I left downstairs alone as it was fully staffed. and put a carvery upstairs with Diane's Dad as the chef. I soon had the place making money. There was Christine who was one of my top waitresses and was very eye catching and a figure you would have to turn and look again. I put her in charge of the drinks and the money. I don't ask ages but I would say 20 at the most. She had slanting eyes as if she had a Chinese Grandma. But it improved her beauty. Her name was Christine. I don't remember how it happened, but I had a furnished apartment that I had for sale close by. I said, would you like to take a ride with me and check out my apartment and perhaps have some sex. She was very willing and the only reason it did not happen again was I didn't think it was a good idea to make out with the staff She was a good lay, every part of her body was firm. Her tits were firm and not an ounce of fat on her. Brendas boy Kerry was still with us and he was a great waiter and very smart. Salvador and his family are going back to Vigo in North Spain. This means 4 people gone who worked for me for 9 years and done a great job. They all lived above the restaurant. The top waiters cooked exotic dishes at the table and they all did silver service at the table. I would never get another chef like Mercedes and another head waiter like Salvador. The vacations I took, If I had done that in America I would have been broke when I returned. I didn't keep the Hayfield long, I sold to our local butcher and made a super profit.

17A

I don't think I would have sold La Tava if Salvador and family had stayed
on. I sold the restaurant back to Houtris the Greek for 6 times what I
paid for it. He didn't run it for long and he became ill and died and the
place fell apart. What a shame, after all the work I put into it. If I had
still been there I think we would still be open. I could handle the staff
better than Houtris. Or it might have meant that I got out at the right
time. We will never know. I was still with Diane after selling La Tava. I
rented a house at Southport, mainly for Clive, he was 17 and he had a girl
friend. I spent a lot oftime at Diane's house and I left Clive to fend for
himself. In 1978 , Yvon got married and I was invited to the wedding and
I took Diane with me, which was probably a mistake. The wedding went
off okay as far as I can remember. Her husband Roy, was a real nice guy.
About this time, Doreen my second wife called and asked if we could get
back together. I said no and that was the last. I heard from her. I would
much sooner have someone that didn't give me any problems. She never
came after me for any money. She was a very independent person. She
did get married again, but it didn't last long. And she had another kid. 3
kids by 3 different men and didn't stay with any of the kids. I think she
just liked them when they were babies. It is now still 1981 and it is the
Christmas holiday and I am taking a short trip to America on my own.
Diane didn't want to go, as she owns a beauty shop and it is her busiest time
of the year. She had already decided that she was not coming to America
with me because of Katrina's education. I suppose she was waiting for me
to pop the question and that would have made a difference. Marriage is
not for me anymore. I Had to go to put a deposit on the new house at
Wellington and I had to chose an R.V. with a tow behind car, so that Clive

and I could go on our tour while we were waiting for the house to be built. I think I was back within a week. Diane wanted to do some improvements to her house. I put in quite a bit of money and finished up owning half the house. After returning from America just after Christmas to Diane's house, I stayed until February of 1982. I wish I had said goodbye to Valerie from Ormskirk and Brenda who was running Silent Seventh. So I leave England with almost a clear conscience. I really treated my first wife and kids bad. I am sorry about that, my second daughter Linda is still not speaking to me. If I had my time over, I would probably do the same, I can't help it. I forgot to mention about the best car I ever had, which I bought about 6 months before selling La Tava.

It was a Lotus Esprit Turbo, Colin Chapman the designer, Designed this car for me. It was white with big red and silver stripes along the body. Even the old ladies would turn their heads as I drove bye. I had it up to 150 m.p.h. on the motor way. Lucky I didn't get caught. I didn't like selling it when I left. Diane and I wrote letters for a while, but it finished when I met Teresa In July of 1982. I was sorry to leave England in a way, but I was looking forward to sunshine every day in Florida.

1

It was 1981 and I was living in England I owned 2 big restaurants and a beautiful big house which was attached to my first restaurant, La Tava which was Greek. It was probably the best 9 years of my life before I came to America. My manager was Spanish and all the rest of the staff were Spanish. I knew nothing about the business but I knew how to manage people. I would help out 3 nights a week when it was busy. The business was already established. I bought it from a Greek. I tripled the size and sold it back to him for almost $500,000 having bought it for $80,000. I did the renovations as an owner builder for $75,000. Most of the staff were getting paid under the table and it is difficult to change a policy that had already been set by a previous employer. It was only the part timers that it applied to. Then I had a visit from the value added tax people, who were as bad as the Inland Revenue for putting a scare into you. They took my books away for a couple of days. Everything was fine. I think it was this that prompted me to sell up and start again. Somewhere nice and warm, I had had enough of the English weather. My other restaurant was an easy sell so then I had to decide. Spain, France, Italy or America. Having been to America before and checked out California and Florida. I decided on Florida because it was closer to home and the property was cheaper. I did not think about the hurricanes, one has earthquakes in California anyway. I went to an exhibition in London and they were marketing. Wellington which was next to West Palm Beach. I liked the set up and eventually bought a house on my arrival in America. I had a lot of stuff to get rid of, so I decided the only way was to have an auction. It really surprised me, some things went for more than anticipated, others went for next to nothing if you want an adventure, go to America, everything is cheaper than Europe. So many things to see and so many opportunities to make money. Go on a B 2 visitor passport. See an attorney when you arrive. Go for an E2 for a business or a green card, which takes longer but allows you to work and you can travel the world without any problems when arriving back in the States. One can always work the Flea markets while waiting. I think as long as you have your application in you are okay, but do not quote me. There are millions of illegal people in America and nobody bothers them. They work in restaurants, farm workers Flea Markets, selling all types of merchandice. Just watch your money, specially in Florida, So many scams. If it sounds to good to be true, it.is probably a scam.

2

Arrived in Florida Feb 1982 on B2 Visa, intending to convert to an E2 visa as soon as the attorney had processed the documentation. My son Clive was with me. He was 18 and was covered under my documents until he was 21. I needed $100,000 to invest in a business. This was no problem as I was a dollar millionaire anyway. Of course the house in. Wellington was about 2 months away from completion, so I thought we would take a little tour of the coast up as far as San Francisco and come back through Arkansas, Alabama, Georgia, and back to Florida. We were on the road for 6 weeks. I bought a brand new Pace Arrow 35 foot motor home. Traded it back to the dealer with a loss of only $2,000, It would have cost me a lot more to rent and everything would not have been squeaky clean. I tried to place an advert in the Palm Beach Post for a couple of girls to come on the trip.They turned me down flat. How times have changed. Read their paper now. I had to buy a Car to pull behind the motor home, it was new but it was only a cheapie. My big mistake was to buy a car without air conditioning. Hey I do not know how hot it gets in a car. I have only just landed on American soil. We stayed at all the best campgrounds. There was one in California where the Jacuzzi was at a temperature of 115 degrees and someone died while we were there. I could not believe the change in the weather. I actually saw ice on the trip back home and was glad to see Florida again.

During this time, a beautiful house was being built. 3 bed 2 bath with pool on the golfcourse, 2 car garage. All the carpet areas were white; and the tiled areas were white; Fully furnished with the finest Italian- furniture. All white so that I can see if there are any bugs. It was time to get rid of the car without air and get something decent. My first choice was a new corvette. Then I had to have one of the big 4 wheel drive jeeps. This was when I met Nancy.She was working part-time at the jeep dealership, she was only 21 and a college grad. I asked her out and she said yes. I had· not had-any sex since leaving England. I took her back to the house which was now complete and had a sample of American hospitality.I think girls are the same all over the world if you play your cards right. I only saw Nancy a few times because I had my eye on somebody else. I was playing golf at the local club and was arranging a tee off time when I noticed this cute little blonde behind the counter. I said to Clive. I am going to have her 105 Ibs with a beautiful body and very pretty. Married but unhappy. Her name was Teresa I had to work very hard before she caved in, then she let me down on a date before we got together on a real date. We met in the morning and eventually finished up at the Rendezvous and had a great time. Good food and good conversation. Then she had to go to work. I was to see her after work. She said I have a surprise for you when you meet me after work. I Was thinking mad passionate love all night, I got a shock, she rolls up with a:joint which I was not used to being from a sheltered part of England. She came back to the house for coffee and never left. Must have been good coffee. The sex was fantastic, I did not need Nancy anymore. I do not use protection and I would be a lot safer with a married woman. I had the vasectomy before I left England.

3

All I had to watch out for was the venera(diseases and I had never heard of aids in I982, We had a great time in those early days, we were booking vacations every other week, it was wonderful. It did not take me long to full in love with Teresa. From that day on I did not need anyone else. I needed to get some type of business going. I had an active mind and had to do something to make some money, One cannot keep spending without having some form of income. Back in the late 70s I was getting about 18% interest on my money, but in the 80s the interest was the pits. So I had to get my brain working again. After all I had moved to America with the intension of opening a restaurant. I was going to buy a piece of land and build it from scratch. I did actually buy an acre of land for this purpose. I never got round to building it. There were so many restaurant going bust, it would have been better to buy one of them. I sold the land many years later to the man who had the adjacent property. In 1983 I rented a store in West Paln Beach and filled it with new video games. This was for Clive, to keep him occupied. The business attracted a rough element and Clive was scared. Next thing I know he is taking one of my guns to work for protection. The police found out and I was in trouble. They did not handcuff me and take me to jail. Just a verbal warning. As soon as I had bought the house I got a Florida driving license, as the insurance was cheaper. I could not wait to buy a load of guns as we were not allowed guns in England. Only one of the guns has been fired and they are all locked away except 2, which are used for home protection. We closed the video store. Too many people were buying videos and running them out of their computers. I got in the business at the wrong time, so I had to sell off the machines one by one. I lined them up all round the porch and after about a year they were gone. Now I have to do something else as the video business was a dead loss. I must be a crazy person. I think I can do anything. After all I was in the restaurant business in England for 9 years. I did not even know the business when I started, but after the 9 years I had made my fortune with enough money to start a new life. It was 1984 and I decided I was going to build a public auto auction. They had them in England, so why not West Palm Beach, I purchased 15 acres of land on Southern blvd. Virgin land covered with weeds and trees. Teresa's Dad, who was in heavy equipment cleared the land. It was a fantastic location and only a couple of miles from the big dealer auction. As it was a commercial project I could not do the construction as an owner builder on the building, but took care of all the interior work including putting the roads in and getting drawings from the engineer to say that our light poles would stand 120 mph wind. I had to change engineers halfway through as he was getting confused. Poor guy, we had such a time with county inspectors I wished I had never started. I finally got the place opened. I had to get a car dealers license before I could start. I already had that organized. I got a lot of dealers coming to the auction. Naturally I ran it on different nights, it would have been silly to have run the same nights as the dealers auction. After a short time, I could tell that we were not going to make it, sold 10 acres to the dealer auction. They used it as a recon center and the other 5 acres to a Real Estate Broker who built storage warehouses. That is what I should have done, my brain has become fuddled since arriving in the States. I did not make any money on the sale, but closing agent deducted $80,000 withholding tax for non U.S. citizens. Can you imagine getting that money back from the I,R,S. It took a while and of course legal expenses. The next business was a beauty shop. I was trained in London as a ladies hairdresser. I knew the business but was unable to work in America because one had to be licensed. Not that I wanted to work anyway as I do not think it is a quick way of making money. This project was for Teresa. She could have her brother Jason working with her. I fitted out the store with all brand new equipment. We were lucky enough to get a good hairdresser from Cuba Things went well for a time, but we had a few problems and we sold out.

4

I Did come over to this country to open a restaurant and along comes a Broker with this fabulous deal, too good to be true of course. He has 2 guys from North Carolina looking for a partner. I was to put in 50% of whatever was required for a 50% share. The good part was that the restaurant was already built and operating. We probably had to pay a brokerage fee. The name of the restaurant was Bobby Robinos and it was situated inside the Sheraton Hotel. We did not have to pay any rent until our gross takings were over $10,000 a month. That seemed a fantastic deal. We had to service the hotel rooms with food. But that was no big deal. The names of my partners were Peter Pons and Gary Triggs. Pons as I soon found out, was one of the worst persons that I had ever met in my life, he was even cheating on Triggs. He was old and ugly and always chasing the skirts and giving out free drinks. He is probably dead now as he would be almost 100 years if still living. Triggs seemed a nice guy but he must have been in on the swindle. I was looking after the banquets and weddings. Pons was looking after the bar and the catering. Triggs was not involved in the running of the business. I put in $400,000 which was supposed to be half of the money required to modernize the restaurant. They kept making excuses. Saying that their money had not come through yet and that they would pay me interest on my money. That did not last long, we were getting into big trouble. We had at least 40 staff and stuff was going out the back door as quick as you could say gone. I do not know for sure who was involved. All I knew is that I could not stand working with that ignorant bastard Pons. anymore. I Went to an attorney in North Paln Beach who wrote up a buy out agreement To cut a long story short he messed up. Pons and Triggs put the whole thing into bankrupsy and came out without any cash input. My total loss was $400,000. Some of the attorneys over here are worse than useless. I shall be suing this guy later. One needs a lot of money to start off again in a new country especially if you are going to live it up like I did and spend money on foolish businesses, I was on an E2 visa for 10 years until I got my green card through marriage to Teresa which happened on Nov 3 1990. I still do not understand why the immigration authorities give us such a hard time when going through customs. We are always together in war and peace, so what is the problem. They made my Son go back to England on his 18th Birthday, or it could have been his 21st I lose track of time over here They wanted to know the time and day of his flight. Clive has a green card now and nobody bothers you when you have a green card, Teresa and I got married in the beautiful house that I had built in Homelands in Lake Worth Florida, I bought a beautiful 5acre piece of land. We had paved road access and it was just what we wanted to build our super house. I built the house as an owner builder but worked it through a contractor for the mane construction, but I worked with all the sub contractors direct. I was tired of the neighbors in Wellington, The houses were so close together and people were so strict, trying to run your life and telling you what to do. The first job on the new property was to dig a lake to get enough fill for the house pad. As the house was so big, we had to dig a lake about 14 foot deep and about 200' wide and 200' long. The fish soon started to arrive. The birds must drop the eggs. No doubt we had snakes in there to. I remember cutting the grass one day, after the place was built and I cut a big cotton mouth right in half; never saw it coming. Glad I was on a riding mower. No alligators , thank you. I was so pleased with the house when it was finished. Including the pool enclosure it was approaching 10,000sq feet. It was okay until I got the property tax bill. After picking myself up, I said to Teresa. We should sell this place. We had at least 4 years in the place. We had some good times in this house. Teresa's brother Jason was a party animal with lots of friends. He was such a great guy. I never heard him say a bad word against anybody. He wouldn't hurt a fly but he was such a lost soul. He did not know what direction to take in life. I loved Jason because of the way he had looked after Teresa. I am sure he taught her a few bad habits, but only little ones, We had so many parties in both houses. I used to go to bed at 2am and leave them to it. Otherwise the next day is shot.

5

Teresa and I got married in the big house. My Real Estate broker at the time was Dannie Biggs. He performed the ceremony. He said to Teresa. Do you Ken, take this woman to be your lawful wedded wife. He got mixed up but everyone had a good laugh. We self catered, but everything turned out good and Dannies wife made the cake. We had 75 guests and we had a really good disc jockey to get everyone in the party spirit. One of our guests read us a poem about love. It was like being in a theater, he read it so well and had all the women in tears. Teresa had finally backed me into a corner. After being together for almost 9 years it is time we got married she said. If you do not marry me I am not staying with you. I want children. It is time. She knew that I had had a vasectomy so what was she on about. I am almost broke, why would you want to marry me now. We have had some good times, so why would you change things. Nothing changes when you get married she said. I reserve my opinion. I said , I had been married twice in England before. Okay I said, I will get the re connection. We will get married and live happily ever after. The re connection did not work. After that we spent months on artificial insemination where one chooses from a sperm bank. She got pregnant once but it never went to term. It might have been Gods choosing. I had 3 other children and if you want my opinion, I was a terrible father. After we sold the beauty shop , Teresa got a job as a receptionist and became very good friends with Rita the owner who became Teresas maid of honor at the wedding. Unfortunately Rita could not work with other hairdressers and Teresa left to work at a big salon in Palm Beach. It was a big shop with about 20 staff and she started in the busy season. She soon became manager and had that salon running like clockwork. She made so many good friends in that shop. I used to enjoy watching her open all the gifts the clients gave to her. All the clients were rich with homes up north and would come down for the season to escape the cold weather up north. Teresa completely changed the place. She would decorate for all the seasons. Something that nobody else had done before. She was happy at the job, most of the time. My green card has to be renewed every 10 years. I have already renewed it once. Teresa is an American citizen of course. I cannot say enough about Teresa. She is a wonderful person. She is pretty and she is good inside, loves children but never had any, thanks to me. The only arguments we ever had was about Clive and he was such a pain in the arse. His mother left him when he was 7. I brought him up as best I could and even now 43 he lays the gilt trip on me. Just tells his girl friends how bad I am. I do not speak to him any more. His mother was sexy and pretty, but I had had enough after 5 years. We were always arguing. She came after me with a knife when she caught me with another woman, but that is another story. We have a lot of pets, the trouble is they do not live long enough. First of all we had a golfin bird that we had for 23 years and we finally had to sell it , because it was driving us crazy with the noise. Then we had twinkle the cat which died mysteriously, It was some poison, but we never found out where it came from. Then we got Booby who was a mix and then brandy a cocker spaniel. They were both good companions. Then we had 2 German Shepards and the cat whose name was Juliet and Amber our outside cat. Too many, but what are you going to do. Just after our wedding, Jason got very depressed, he was gay and things were not going to good for him. He took too many pills, crying out for attention. Unfortunately nobody was there to save him. He gambled with his life and lost A tragic loss to friends and family. He was also a brilliant hairdresser. Teresa missed him so much and to this day has not got over it.

6

Lets talk about health insurance and life insurance. Health insurance is
not too expensive when one is young and does not need it. As one gets
older, the insurance company will not insure preexisting conditions. So
what are you going to do. My agent advised me to lie about my age.
They will never catch it he said. They caught me and I was lucky to get
paid, but only a small portion of the claim. It satisfied the doctors, so it
got them off my back. I tell you what is great about being sick with no
insurance. One can walk , or be carried into a Hospital emergency room
and they must admit you. They will send you a bill but will not enforce
it Every one must have life insurance, but who can afford it. Teresa and I
have been paying a little over $1,400 a year for the past 10 years. Now it
is going up to $9,000 this year. I do not think I will be a participant. I
have come across a lot of people taking drugs in America. It is probably
the same in England, but I suppose that the people that I hung out with
did not do it, so I did not think they existed, Jason and Teresa liked to do
their pot. At parties they used to pass joints round to their friends and they
would take hits off the same joint I could not believe Teresa would, as she
is normally very hygienic. I loved her for what she was and did not try to
change her. She liked her pot and champagne. She eventually got away
from the pot as it went sky high in price.I never forget when we went to
Jamaica one vacation. One guy was selling joints like cigars for $5 bucks
a pop. He said, did we want to buy 5 acres of pot. We are not that crazy.
Another time Teresa bought a bag of pot from somebody on the beach
and it turned out to be seaweed, I am glad she did not get into the hard

drugs where one had to shoot up. I do not drink and I do not do drugs. How boring, but I did not need alcohol to give me a lift as I was always the same with no ups or downs. Teresa thinks I show no emotions. The only thing wrong with me is I need 2 knee replacements. I can not walk very far and I have to take pain pills every day, I was bowling 4 nights a week in 4 different leagues. As my legs got worse I just had to give it up. My average in one league was 178. *Liked golf too but it was too expensive to go too. often.Introduced Teresa to golf and she was a natural. We do not play much, but she always plays well* when we do. She is such a hard worker too. Can not sit still for 5 minutes. Always on the go. Her birth sign is the crab and she always likes to be in the pool, The water has to be the right temperature for me. Teresa has a grandma in a nursing home in North Carolina who is 103 and Teresa telephones her every night. Teresa is 28 years younger than me and when I first met her, I told her I was 35, but I was actually 52. It was my son that told on me. I have always looked 20 years younger, No one has ever said to me. Could you introduce me to your daughter. I did have a face lift at 53 to tighten up the loose flesh, which was an improvement But have not had another since. I have one daughter 6 months younger than Teresa and one a little older. They both live in England and are both married. Yvon my eldest visits us every other year which started the year 2000 and Linda wants nothing to do with me because I walked out on them. Yvon contacted my brother in the mid nineties and told him that she would like to start talking and writing to us. Teresa got on well with Yvon and eventually we visited her and her husband Roy in 1997 a month after Princess Diane died. Roy was the greatest, he would do anything for us. So glad Yvon appears to be happy. I am very proud of my son Clive, because he has done well for himself, but we can not seem to hit off, so we have lost contact and have not spoken for 2 years. I wish Roy and Yvon would move to America. Roy would, but Yvon Has to look after her Son who is about 19. I built a house for Clive in 1991 at a cost of $82,000 and today it is worth about $300,000. He was always complaining about the house. I did not pay cash but set him up with a mortgage that he could afford. 18 years old and the house still looks light brand new. Best house in the area, but thats not a good thing when you want to sell. I decided to get myself a Real Estate licence in 1988 because the money was going fast and I needed a back up. It only took me 2 weeks and I had passed the State exam. Any test I have taken

I have always passed first time. I had passed my Pilots license in England and I transferred to America with about an hour check out. All countries except a British license. In 1998 I studied for the Auctioneers license which I passed first time. I also trained in London to be a ladies hairdresser and it has been very handy throughout the years.

7

It is only recently that I have admitted my age to anyone but I am sure close friends and relatives knew all the time. I was only fooling myself. Yvon my first born is older than my wife. Linda my second daughter is 6 months younger than Teresa. Clive was from my second wife. It has been a long time since I have communicated with any of my children from my first marriage. Then out of the blue my brother Chris from England called me and said Yvon would like to get in touch with me. It was then that we started talking on the telephone. Teresa got on well with Yvon and they became instant buddies. We eventually went to England to visit them and of course to show Teresa the sights of London, Yvon's husband Roy is a fantastic guy, he just could not do enough for us. Ten years later he is still the same. We were in London just after Princess Diana died. The flowers were everywhere, it was such a tragedy. We all went to visit my brother Chris and his wife Sandra. Who had already visited us in our Wellington house in 1984. So they knew Teresa. They never came back again, I do not think they like flying as they always have their vacations in England at the seaside. Chris was the best pool cleaner we ever bad. He kept the pool spotless while he was there. Linda does not want anything to do with me so there is nothing I can do about that. I should have taken Teresa across the tunnel to France and showed her Paris, but time seemed to fly and we never got round to it. There are so many things to see in London. The bridges the thames, Cathedrals, Buckingham Palace, different exhibitions, We took so many pictures, Also Madam Tusards. It was a joy to me to have some of My favourite foods that I can not get in America. It had been 15 years since I bad been to England and there are always things one misses from home. I say to Teresa, we should live in

England and take advantage of the National Health. No thanks it is too cold. Funny she shonld say that. The only cold I have had in the last 50 years was in 1997 when we went to England. Roy likes America so much, He would like to live here. Yvon does not want to leave her son who is about 21. I know she likes to come and see us as she comes every other year and is now going to come every year. Roy is a help and always wants to do jobs in the house and round the yard. We hired a car and I showed Teresa all the places I had lived, where I was born and all the places that I had had my businesses including my restaurants. We had a good time but Teresa has not wanted to go back, For our vacations we usually choose the exotic places. Nadine my first wife was a sweet pretty girl who never remarried and never forgave me for leaving them. Those were my young and reckless days and I am sorry. But I can not turn back the clock. My Son Clive hates me, he blames me for everything that goes wrong in his life. He has no respect for me. He calls me an old fart. Which does not bother me, but Teresa hates it. His Mother left him when he was 7 and I have tried to bring him up good. I should have done the same as his mother. I am sorry to say that the only thing I have done well at in the U.S.A is Real Estate and I always have done good at that even in England. Thanks Donald Trump, but your advice came too late for me.

8

My first days with Teresa were something else. They were so great. One could say that she was the love of my life and it would be true. We had vacations planned every other week. Teresa had to give up work. We went to New York in November of 82. We stayed at a Howard Johnson Hotel on one of the busy streets for 1 week and did all the sights. I had been to New York before on a tour from England, so I knew what to show Teresa The weather was a little colder than Florida, so we had to take winter clothes. I had a full length leather coat that I had purchased in Morocco 20 years ago and it still looked like brand new. I had only worn it a couple of times. The drinks were expensive. But we did not know where to go for the best deals. We were walking along Broadway and all of a sudden a man dropped right in front of us. Looked like someone had scattered 40 pound of hamburger meat all over him. It was all his guts that had been spewed out all over the pavement. Someone had shot him at close range. Teresa said. I am not coming here again, We did not get a lot of sleep, the sirens kept us awake all night. One had to go and visit Empire State Building and the Statue of Liberty. The rest of the time , I am sure we spent the rest of the time making mad passionate love. Oh yes we did take a ride on the horse and buggy. We went to dinner at the top of the world, about 100 floors. The views were great and so was the meal but we had to order a pizza when we went back to the hotel and I am sure we spent at least $300. On my previous trip I had bought some expensive ornaments, but unfortunately they got stolen from our house in 1991. February of 1983 we decided to go to Hawaii. We stayed at a beautiful hotel in Owaho and also visited Kerwaui. We had such a great time, we said we would like to stay and open a business, but we never did. It is such an awkward place to

9

On the Real Estate there was one exception, which was Teresa's sister Linda. She trusted me and I bought 2 pieces of land which she hadn't even seen and I also sold her property down in South Florida for $430,000 and somebody had had it on the market 5 years and I sold it in 2 months. Teresa sometimes says to me. I wish we still lived in the Wellington house. Tom and Regis next door were nice people, but they always had to interfear. We put the Christmas tree out for garbage a day early. Knock nock who's there. He did become the mayor you know. They acted 30 years older than what they were. I wonder what they looked like now, Our other neighbor was completely different. Ted and Pat were their names with 2 children. The girl was about 15 and she was hot. I said to Clive, this was about 1983 you have to go for her, but he didn't know how. He hadn't been watching me over the years. Ted was into vending machines and I think Pat was classified as a housewife. She had a terrible accident with a gas grill and she was badly burned, she was such a nice person. My son Clive takes after my brother Chris who went from a young boy to a man. He seemed to miss the chasing of the girls period. The teenage years where one chases all the girls was missing in his life and I think he married the first girl he dated. Her name was Sandra, who is a very nice person and always makes me welcome whenever I see her, which is not very often since we are now living in America. Chris and I worked at Odhams Press in Watford Hertfordshire printing the magazine runs. We both had to serve apprenticeship, but the Company closed down and everybody had to relocate. My brother is 13 years younger than me. We love Chris and Sandra and their 2 children very much, and it is such a pity that we can't see them more often. I remember our first trip to Jamaica which I mentioned earlier. We went on this boat trip down the river. I remember we had lots of fun and everybody was happy and singing. Of course they were serving Rum runners which was included in the price, so everybody was drunk. When the boat stopped, we got off the boat and first thing Teresa said was, I gotta pee, so she went to the side of the road and lifted up her skirt and peed. My little cutie was prettier than any filn star and I have the photos to prove it with her perfect body and her pretty face. We were so happy that we were soon very much in love which has so far lasted 26 years. My record before that was about 7 years with previous wives and long time girl friends. Getting back to Jamaica, we had such a great time, on the beach, tours on the island. Making love all night. As they say, youth is wasted on the young. As one gets older, one makes appointments in the mind that the body can't keep. Teresa didn't like flying and had to have a few drinks before taking off. We visited Las Vegas twice and really had a great time, we go for the excitement of the place, the lights the cheap buffets and the best shows in the world and just to get away. How a place can change in 10 years. One used to get into the shows for next to nothing. We stayed in the same hotel which was the Flamingo. Aruba was the last of our flying trips. We had a great time as usual. Same old stuff beach and pool and checking out the stores and flea markets. Just being together anywhere in the world. We didn't argue, that is what made it so nice to be together was wonderful.

10

To give an illustration of how fussy I used to be about a girls weight. One must think I am very vain. That would be true. This girl worked for a newspaper and was trying to sell me advertising. To cut a long story short, I dated her. On the first night I ran my hands over her body and figured her weight to be 112 lbs, which is quite acceptable. She was gorgeous, educated with her own beautiful house and only 15 miles away. Looked as if she had money too. After 3 months she had put on 30 lbs. I had to say goodbye. When making love to a woman I don't like to feel wobbly fat I was talking to a black man and he said that most of his kind preferred women that had a bit of fat on them. Takes all sorts to make the world go round.During our 26 years together we have done a lot of cruising. The ideal vacation if you don't like flying and you can drive to the port. Do they get you on the parking fees. Some travel agencies ferry you down to the port at no charge, and pick you up. We have been on about 25 cruises. We like to go to the different ports and look around. We have probably visited almost every habitable island in the Caribbean and we do the Same old stuff which never gets boring because of the person you are with. We always visit the stores for our perfume and the booze. We never miss the flea markets, Then it is time to relax on the beach. We sometimes go on a tour on the island. If you can get another couple it is much cheaper to hire a car. I don't advise hiring a scooter. They seem to have a lot of accidents. There are a lot of mad drivers on some of the islands. The ships are so nicely fitted out, we try to go for the new ships that are coming out. Everything is much fresher and we hope, better design giving us more room in the cabin. We enjoy dressing up for dinner and being waited on.Living in Florida, one does not dress up as much as living in a cold climate, just jeans and tea shirts. Our best cruise was on the Grand Princess to the Mediterranean and visited Portugal, Spain, Italy, France. We went to see the Pope, we were lucky as it was the 25 year jubilee and there was all sorts of demonstrations and people were going wild. We did hear the Pope speak so that was good. We picked up all sorts of crosses from the Vatican City, they were so cheap, I wish we had got more. We took a lot of video as there was so much to see inside the cathedral. We also visited the leaning tower of Pizza. We took so many tours on this trip as the towns were so far from the ports. This was a long cruise with an outside cabin which wasn't cheap. But you only live once, which is Teresa's favorite saying. However she is not wasteful with money and inclines to buy things when they are 70% off. We had to fly back from Barcelona which was a pain. Celebrity Cruise Lines and Royal Caribbean and Princess would be our best choices for the mature cruiser. All the cruise ships have good food and good entertainment All you have to spend is for your drinks which are expensive and they give you a card so that you pay at the end of the cruise. Of course one spends more when one is not parting with the green stuff. We always take 8 bottles of champagne in a case and the last cruise which was on the Norwegian Pearl they said if we wanted to drink them on board we would have to pay a corkage fee of $15 a bottle. We only paid $5.95 a bottle so I said, you keep it. We got it back 2 days later. They didn't know what they were doing. We always like to get a 14 day cruise as a 7 day goes too quick. We have to put our two German Shepards in the kennels, but they are together, two bitches, sounds awful and Lady looses weight but she soon puts it back on when we come home. They are Teresa's dogs for sure, I am just an also ran or a feeding machine. So long as they do not bite me, its okay. Never even growled at me. They are good guard dogs and they are in the house with us. Not chained to a tree like some dogs are.

11

I learnt Judo in England when I was 29 years old and I only got as far as blue belt, But it was a confidence builder and throughout my life if I have ever fallen I cushioned my full because of my training I was taught by a 6th Dan black belt. Who was one of the best in England and I had the 1 on 1 training. I used to go just after beauty school training as it was in London and it was 20 miles away.I was opening a beauty salon close to home. My brother trained for judo also, but it was closer to home with a big class. I opened the beauty shop and it was my intention to put in a manager to run the place. Everyone wanted the owner to do their hair. I got out of there as I could earn better money at the printing. By the way, I did meet my second wife there and she was a fantastic hairdresser. She could cut and roll a perm in 20 minutes. My beauty school training was never a waste of time. My hair was grey at 29 and I have colored it ever since. I have still plenty of hair and Teresa cuts it every couple of weeks as she is a good Hairdresser. I do the Bleach work on her hair and it always looks nice. It has saved us a lot of money over the years. I have never had a woman leave me, Which goes to show, I know how to treat a woman. I suppose I have always been a ladies man and have always had at least 2 girlfriends at a time. If you get rid of one, there is always a spare until you find another. Of course they don't find out and I have always had good health and been able to keep everybody happy. Since meeting Teresa I have not had the need for anyone else, which is good, so you don't have to keep lying.Let me tell you about the worst scam of all. Because this couple had become our best friends. We met them on a cruise and became friends. I have always been able to make money, but I was unable to hang on to it. Teresa and I met Lauri Hurwich and his wife Maryann.

Who appeared to like us. We did not have many friends and when they started inviting us down to their house every other week. I thought I might learn something from this guy as he said he was a financial adviser. He said that he was putting a deal together with the Indians in Phoenix Arizona to build a Hi li and did I want to come in with. Him. He was in the final stages and I would make Millions. All he wanted right now was $50.000 and I would be a partner. Crazy, greedy me fell for it. With my money he hired a boat for his 40th birthday to take us all down the intra coastal on a dinner cruise and champagne too., He kept asking for more money and I gave it to him. After all a friend is not going to screw me for money. I finished up giving him over $200,000 unsecured. Goodbye money. What goes around comes around, he even screwed his brother for money. I was fast running out of money and one needs money to make money. I don't have friends anymore thanks to situations like this, only acquaintances. Then there was the man from England who was looking for $25,000 to extend his business. He went bankrupt and wiped out my $25,000. I can't believe how stupid I was. I am so sharp now I wouldn't lose a dime or lend a penny. I still have another couple of worms to report. Eddy Dayanoff and Lucky. Two of the biggest slime balls in West Palm Beach. Dayanoff owned a couple of pawn shops and he come up with this idea about lending money on car titles and was looking for an invester. Lucky who knew me from Bobby Robinos introduced me. I should have known as he had shifty eyes. You know what I mean, he couldn't look you in the eyes. With all their sins I am sure they are both dead. I was to keep the titles as my security. Things were not working out with the titles not always being available at the store and I foolishly let them have them. Within a few days Dayanoff ordered me out of the store and said I was trespassing and he would call the police if I didn't go What option did I have. It was now a civil matter. Another $150,000 including my 5 carat flawless diamond ring which I brought over from England. I employed a firm of attorneys from West Palm to take my 4 cases totaling about a million bucks. My attorneys name was Tom Hoadley from Hoadley and Noska. Every time he got up to speak, I winced. Words cannot describe how useless he was. All he got me was $45,000. If he is still alive, he should be selling vegetable at Lake Worth flea market. I could have done a better job. Having lost my money I had to start making some money. Having passed the State Real Estate test I was ready to go but passing the test does not show you how to make money in Real Estate. Only 20% make the real money in the business and the other 80% either give it up or just make a little. I still had some money and a small house. I started with Gwen Burge but soon moved on to Fabulous Homes, Dannie Biggs being the owner ,the man that did our wedding. I tried to get in on the ocean Real Estate companies but no one would talk to me. It took me 3 years before I had made a name for myself before I was accepted to the Palm Beach Board which covered the ocean properties. Shortly after, Dannie Biggs stopped talking to us. I never to this day found out why.

12

On the outskirts of town, lets say a property sells for $75,000 Let us say a property in a better area sells for $300,000 It takes the same amount of work and people buying the more expensive property can usually get financing a lot easier. The agents make more money with more expensive properties. I moved around the Companies in the ocean area to get experience. Then I went to Orlando to study for the auctioneers license which I passed first time. Then I went to National Auction to get hands on experience, but I soon left as I never got to be the Auctioneer so that was no fun. I went with a smaller Company. Then on to my next learning curve. I joined Ronald Lawrence in West Palm to learn how to sell businesses. I had to pay $250 for the tuition. I was already good at selling businesses but I thought lets see what the experts say, because that is all they did. We soon parted.

I got a listing Rvs and all the stuff that went with it. He was only netting about $150,000 but he wanted a $1,000,000 which I admit was a little high and what Ron had suggested, $700,000 was nearer the mark. He refused to budge on the price and I lost the listing.If it was my call, I would have listed it and dropped the price at a later date. After leaving, I called to see the seller after 2 months and he had already sold to a big company in Fort Lauderdale. In my early days of Real Estate I snapped my Achilles tendon. They put a full length cast on my leg and in weeks it selfhealed, isn't that amazing how the body does that After 18 years it is stronger than my left leg. I had a great time at Hampton Real Estate, which was only 200 yds from the ocean in Manalapan. Big beautiful office and right next to Teresa's salon where she worked for 12 years. Eventually the broker had to move her office as the rent went up to high. She relocated to Ocean Ridge, She had a boy named Ken from New York who was always calling her. I am glad she has settled down now and is engaged. Another thing I did was to advertise in an English newspaper, for people to emigrate to the States to live and set up a business. Two couples came together who were related, but I only managed to satisfy and locate one couple.The other couple were not adventurous and went back to England. So we have Graham and Irene. I put them in a Blockbuster type store in a good location. After a couple of years they sold out to Blockbusters and got their Green cards.Graham got himself a crew and did yard work Irene either worked in a bank or as a mortgage broker. She had her boobs done and used to get them out to show how nice they were. She was pretty hot and She gave Clive a lot of opportunities and I know he didn't do anything. Graham encouraged him. They moved to Key West and Graham died at about 55. I wonder what Irene is doing today. Clive had more contact with them than we did and used to help out sometimes on the lawn maintenance. Clive has had no contact with his mother since 1988. We told him that he could go back home or we would rent him a place at his expense. We would put up first last and security and give him some furniture. He hated us from that moment. 15 years later he thanks us. It made a man of him (I think) He has no idea about health situations. It took him 20 years to go to the dentist. When I was 52 I looked about 30. Thats how I got away with chatting up the young broads. On most of the cruises we went on and our other vacations before we were married I had such a hard time with customs. I think they didn't understand what an E 2 visa was. One time they said that I would have to report to INS within 7 days. Of course I never did and this was before all the terrorist scares, Every time we went through Teresa was so scared I think she was filling her pants. When I got my green card because of the marriage, it was a lot better and no more trouble. She always thought that they were going to deport me. Watch out you guys from England. Make sure your papers are in order. No one told the INS that we were good friends with America. Another way to get a permanent residence in America. Lets say that you are a Greek chef living in England. A Greek restaurant opens, but they can't get a chef. Take the job and you are in America to stay.

13

I think I became a changed person when I met Teresa. When I look back, remembering how badly I treated my first wife. I was so cruel, Yet she was a beautiful girl and when I look back remembering how nice she was. She did nothing to warrant me walking out on the whole family. Teresa says to me, don't you feel guilty, I don't know how you could have done what you did. If I thought about it I would feel guilty I just wiped it out of my memory bank. Teresa and I never get into a fight or argue, and if we do it is about Clive or her family. I love them all. Annette the middle sister, would give you her last dime. She works heavy equipment at a junk yard. She is always in pain with her legs. She is living 200 mls away, but is always a joy to see her. Linda the older sister I relocated to an upgraded trailer park after the sale of her house. She is very happy where she is and she is still working. Looking after the elderly who require private nursing. I miss Teresa's family as if they were mine. In my later years I love everybody even the American Cops. Most of which in the smaller counties would sooner tazor you rather than help. You don't get the bully cops in England, Brits beware, when in America, keep your tongue in your mouth and keep it shut or regret for the rest of your life. Having said that I know there are good and bad everywhere but the English cops don't carry guns. So one could finish up dead which would ruin your holiday. I still love America, you just have to be in the right place at the right time not the wrong place at the wrong time. There are more opportunities here. The weather is better, if you choose the right State. I could become an American citizen, but I haven't bothered and that means I can not vote or do jury duty. But have to renew my green card every 10 years. Perhaps I will do it when it is getting close to the ten years, I treat people as I would like them to treat me. I am not a snob and I will converse with the lowest of the low. I heard about Vocational Rehab from Annette so I decided to check it out. They were going to get both my knees done so that I could go to work. I was 75 years old at this time. They sent me to Doctor Risch for exrays and a report. Next thing that I hear, An inspector from the State is coming over to evaluate me and 3 college kids. We were given alsorts of maths tests. Something I was used to 64 years ago. I still remembered but was a little slower than I would have liked. I found out later that it was an IQ test which was my first. They said it was above average and extremely high for my age. It wasted over 4 hours of my time, because they said I was too old to work and they probably caught me out on a couple of white lies. I could have appealed, but I didn't. I was pretty clever in most subjects, I took after my mother who was in a wheelchair at the age of 40 due to a displacement of a bone in her spine which had attached to the nervous system. To move it would have been very risky. She was probably dropped at birth. She died at the age of 71 of double pneumonia My father stood by her all his life and died at 68 of cancer of the bowels If I could have got a letter from a Real Estate Broker saying that I needed my knees doing so that I could work, but I asked the wrong guy and he ignored me.

14

I have lived here 26 years. Never regretted leaving England. That was just another chapter of my life. In my mind I have lived 4 lives. Three in England and 1 in America. One with my first wife. One with my second wife. Then one by myself and then one with Teresa. So much land over here, with room to breathe. Buy your own hunting ground in North Florida. Buy as a group, say 1,000 acres at 2,000- 5000 an acre depending on location. Later on you might get a change of zoning to building land and sell for $20,000 an acre. It has happened in the past. You might want to buy a small lot for retirement. Buy land on the water, it always goes up in value. If your home is in England, try a vacation in Florida and if you like it, buy that hunting land. Hunt deer, wild boar and whatever. I have never been hunting in my life, so what do I know. It would impress your friends if you told them that you owned a hunting ground. One can buy almost any kind of gun or crossbow in America. Put up a small shack on your land and then you have an address. Avoid hurricanes from June-November, but they move slow and one can out run them. We don't get them every year, During my 26 years only Andrew came close. Nothing to be scared of, snakes and alligators keep out of your way unless you go looking for them.Best place in the world for a vacation and I would say that one feels safe over here.You have to go to Disney World and Epcot center in Orlando plus many more attractions throughout Florida. The attractions are unbelievable. But expensive if you have a load of kids. Plus every day is a sunshine day, well nearly every day. Gas prices keep going up, but we still have the cheapest gas in the World, so visitors don't worry when they fill their tanks as they have been used to paying more where they live, Lets talk about buying a new car, truck, van in America. If you want to get it at the best price, it is going to take you about 5 hours. First you talk to the salesman and if you like the car, he lets you drive it. Then we make a low ball offer to feel them out. Would you buy this car right now at this price. Would you give us a deposit and drive the car away today. Yes Mr. Salesman. Off he goes to his manager and comes back with a counter offer, about $500 below sticker price. You would be getting it for our costs he says. Car salesmen have a reputation in this country, You make another offer, they turn it down. You start walking out the door and if they don't call you back you know that the vehicle was unobtainable at that price, so you chip in another couple of hundred and you have made the deal. Now we have to deal with the finance guy. Get the rate from your bank first. Then work the finance guy to get a better rate. They give you a free tank of gas when you buy a new car. I don't know when that started. The American cars are a lot more reliable now. In the 80s and 90s we leased about 5 Nissan maximas and we never had to take one back to the shop, so Nissan was our favorite for many years. The best all round vehicle we had was a Ford Expedition. It had 4 wheel drive and every option one could think of. It was an S.U.V and it only did 10 miles to the gallon. Cars are half the price that they are in England. There are so many people moving to Florida, I think it is going to sink into the ocean. We are not much above sea level. It does vary from place to place. If you dig a hole in your back yard you will probably hit water at 8-10 feet. If you are going to move to Florida and you still need to work. You must live close to the big towns or cities, because if you move to the country the wages are the pits, but car insurance is about half. Orlando is probably the best because it has all year round trade. The other cities are seasonal. We always go to the flea markets whenever we can. The best being the one on Sunrise blvd in Fort Lauderdale it takes 2 days to see it all and is a drive in Theater weekdays. They have a new section and a used section. They also have a circus, we go on a Sunday, it is about a 50 mile trip for US when we lived at West Palm. We never go to the Mall as it is too expensive and do our shopping at Super Walmart, Sams, Lowes, Publix, Home Depot, Costco and the dollar stores. and the A.B.C stores for Teresa's champagne. After 26 years I have still got my English accent, which is a plus. Clive lost his accent very quickly. If you are thinking of coming to America, make sure that all the money you bring over is insured. Your account is only covered for $100,000.

15

I went into another business, selling cars I would buy cars from people privately and at the auction Fix them up and resell them. We had already opened up a detail shop for Clive. He was getting cars from other dealers in town. We found the labor force was unreliable and found that it was not paying off, so we closed it down. I couldn't make any money at the various things I went into. If only I had stuck to Real Estate I would not be in this mess. We stayed in the big house for a few months after the Auction. The lady that bought it with her husband could see that Teresa was upset losing the house. She said do not worry, everything is going to be alright. They leased it to us for a very low rent, they decided that it was not for them and they put it back up for sale. In the mean time I was getting another house ready for us, but it was only a 1,000 square feet. We had been in about a month and we were just having the alarms hooked up but not connected to the central station. People heard the alarm but nobody took any notice. We only got paid a fraction of what we lost from the insurance co, Teresa lost a lot of jewelry that I had bought for her. She was very upset, but at least we got something back. We stayed in that house for about 5 years and then we moved to a bigger house just a short distance away that I had built. The area was a little better. We didn't have any robberies at this house. This was the last house we lived in before we left Palm Beach County. There is one thing about moving so much to new houses, we didn't have to paint or renew appliances.It was 2003 and I went to have my knees checked by a Palm Beach doctor. He said that he did not know how I was still able to walk It was bone on bone and I needed the operation. I was managing with pain pills and I could walk short distances but they were getting worse. I got into another business from the house before heading away from Palm Beach County. This couldn't go wrong. Listen to this Buy 20 vending machines. Fill them up with candy and take out the money once a month. About $2,000 a month I think that is what the advertising said. People do not lie in print do they? That might work if you could get your machines in places like an Airport and busy areas I am dreaming again, $10,000 down the drain I was lucky to pull in $300 a month. I sold out for $3,000. Then I lost all the money on the bulk candy. I can only make money in Real Estate, when will I learn. It is January 2003 and we have decided that Palm Beach is getting too busy for us and it would be nice to live in the country for a change. Only thing was, Teresa had a good job and she liked being the boss and organizing everything. The rent was going up and business was bad. I said to Teresa, that shop is not going to last. I was right, it changed hands twice in 5 years. So I set off on my own, because Teresa was working at the Beauty Shop. I headed North to find us a new home. I arrived in Orlando. I said there are some nice places on the outskirts, what do you think? Teresa said lets go further North. I finished up in Interlachen the City of lakes. I found a nice 2 acre lot on a pretty big lake.Prices were low at the time and I got a good deal. My intentions were to build a really nice house. About 4,000 square feet. I had to get something to live in while I was building the house. I couldn't put Teresa in a dump, I thought the best was a mobile home. I bought a nice one, it was 2,300 square feet. I put it on a 1 acre lot about 5 miles East of Hawthorne. We were actually 5.5 miles East of the town. We moved up on the 4th July 2003. Of course the electricity was not on. Something to do with inspections. We finished up staying 4 nights in a Gainesville Motel We had been packing our stuff for a couple of months and it took 2-50 foot trucks To move us. Teresa likes her do dabs and the bigger our house the more she gets.

16

We had to get a 14x30 shed and an awning for our 2 vehicles' We fenced the whole acre with cheap farm fencing & put in a 16 foot farm gate. Then we put a little sod round the front and back and then we were in business. We did not sod the whole area. It would have been too much. My idea was to encourage people to move from South Florida to North Florida. It didn't work. Property was a lot cheaper, but I think there was more to do and wages were better in places like Orlando and West Palm Beach and we had to travel 30 miles to Gainesville and 45 miles to Ocala for the big stores, which was a pain in the butt. I think we made a financial mistake at times, but it is nice living in the country. It is so quiet and the air is so fresh. Our 2 German shepards love it and we feel so safe. If we go out, we leave the dogs in the house. We have not bothered about an alarm. We have a sign on the gate that says we can get to the gate in 5 seconds, can you, and a picture of a German shepard. They are almost human and they know every word we say. We got a little bored after a while and once again, stupid me decides to open a business selling electric and gas scooters and A.T.Vs. And go karts. We didn't even have good sales at Christmas, so I knew it was not going to work. I shipped them off, what I had left to a local boat store and over a period of about 6 months he got rid of them all. So I didn't loose much this time. Only my time and labor. I could not afford to build the house on the Lake, so now I am stuck in the Mobile home. I am glad I got a nice one. We eventually added a pool and now the place is like paradise. We even have signs, this way to paradise on the back deck, I went into a lot of businesses in England and everything was good, and of course the 2 restaurants were super good. The trouble is, I think I can make money easy, but I can't any more. Except with Real

Estate. The next couple of years we took it easy, we had our vacations, we visited family and time flew by. Then came the terrible time It was May 24th 2005 when everything was turned upside down. Let us go back a couple of weeks before the dreadful day. I was getting these flashes of light and messages were coming to me from above. Thinking back I can only assume that God was talking to me. Now I am not a religious person. I wasn't getting any sleep and eating and drinking very little. I do not go to church, only special times like Christmas and Easter and a show from the local church about the crucifiction and how Jesus was born and all that good stuff. My wife is the religious one, she prays every night and thanks God every day for her existence. I do pray but not every day. and I do believe in God. Anyway I was getting these messages every night for about 2 weeks. Get off your arse out of retirement. I was 75 at the time, but I had a terrific amount of energy. I do not know where this energy was coming from, all of a sudden. The message was, in 5 years you will become a billionaire. I want you to go and make peace in the world. Stop all of our soldiers from getting killed in this terrible war against terrorism and our occupation in Iraq. President Bush should never got this country involved. It must have been something to do with the oil. He is certainly doing a good job at Bankrupting us. I can't wait for the elections. Then I said to myself, why would God choose me to do his bidding. I am not a follower of the church, and then it hit me. I am a professional person who is honest and could carry out his wishes. I had spent time since 1988 making little money but learning from 15 or more Real Estate Companies Throughout Florida. Learning their methods. I did not have to make money. I was a millionaire when I arrived in Florida. I didn't have expensive tastes, so I didn't need a lot of money, I had lived a full life in England I was practically unknown and I just moved about quietly learning and doing my business I went by the Realtor code of ethics and always told the truth when dealing with clients. I told my wife during this period and approaching the terrible day. I was going to make her very rich. A pretty broad statement, No wonder she thought I was crazy. It was my Son's birthday the 23rd of May, It was his 41st birthday. He was traveling from West Palm to Hawthorne to spend two or three days with us. He brought his Cuban girl friend with him. I guess he had to have some company. His standards had certainly dropped since leaving England. He drove a new Dodge Magnum which he had borrowed from his boss and it was pearl white, the color I wanted, But not destined to get. Clive was good at what he did. He would sell about 20 top line cars a month through the internet and working through a top car dealer. It was his presentation top line photographs that did it. It is unfortnnate that we do not communicate anymore, because I do love him, and I am proud of his achievements. Even when car dealers were struggling he maintained his average and he was an asset to his boss. Cars and computers that is all.

17

I was working at the Real Estate office earlier that day and was excited about Clive coming down to see us. I was working at doing an auction for the company at the time. It was to take place at Melrose. I was an experiment to see if Real Estate Auctions on small properties would work in North Florida. The broker said it would not work. I said that I could produce a plan that would work. It was a beautiful little house with a barn and a swimming pool. All on 5 acres on a paved road access. I was sure that I would get a good price for it. Everything had been renewed except the barn. It was listed at $169,900 in the M,L,S, and nobody showed it. The Auction did take place on June 25th 2005 The highest bid was $100,000 and the place was packed. A beautiful color brochure and a nicely presented Auction. We did advertise the house in the Buyers Guide and actually got a full price offer before the Auction but I wanted to try the Auction. It does bring it to the attention of people looking to buy and I hadn't done one for a while. I wanted to make sure that the brochure was correct and I wasn't breaking any laws. The broker said he would pay for the Auction but if it sold then the cost was mine, as I did have an interest in the property. The offer was accepted and the woman had 100% mortgage. We did have some problems however and we had to up the price $5,000 to give back to the buyer for closing costs. It is a good job the property appraised for $175,000 because the woman and her horses had already moved in. Most of the Auctions I have done, with the big sign on the property and all the display advertising I do, makes potential buyers aware of the property being for sale and if they don't buy at Auction, they sometimes buy later. People go away from the Auction and then it hits them. I should have bought it, it was a steal. When we sold our house in

Lake Worth to move North we moved at the wrong time, as we could have got double the price for it in 2005. I knew those prices were crazy and it couldn't last, and sure enough people could not afford their mortgages and are in serious trouble right now. The influx of people into Palm Beach County from 2003 to 2005 is unbelievable. I was traveling at 45 mph the speed limit and the flow of traffic was 60mph. I was there in 2005 for a short spell and I would only go out at night, it was terrible. Now it is 2008 and what I forecast has come true, people bought houses they could not afford and now they are up the creek without a paddle and the property market is shot and America is in a hell of a state. I don't know what to do myself. I am frightened of buying properties because I do not know what is going to happen in the future. How long is it going to be before we are back to normal. Getting back to the worst day of life. My Son arrived at 5pm on the 23rd of May 2005 at 5pm. Welcomed him with all the normal hugs and kisses and welcomed his girlfriend too. Settled them in the guest room of our house. Teresa was looking after them, but I was working on ideas to make Teresa rich. I had two or three ideas that I was working on and had a multitude of papers scattered everywhere, I told them that I would talk to them later. I had so many ideas that were coming to me, I thought from God. That I had to get them down on paper. I wasn't eating or drinking. I was working furiously. I told my son Clive to go to bed and I will meet with you at 10am. I said, do you want to join me in a money making scheme or do you want to stay in West Palm 280 miles away and do your own thing. Do not disturb me as I will be working on ideas and I will see you in the morning. I had the office full of papers. I did not want him to see them and I knew he would be snooping around so I taped up the office door and put a sign up. No Entry. I did not sleep all night and I knew he had been nosing around as all the tape was broken. I was mad and told everybody to get out including Teresa until I had finished my paperwork. I put signs on the gates, Keep Out. They all thought I had gone crazy. What really activated the issue was what happened later.

18

First of all a policeman from Putnam County came to see me. Is everything okay Sir, only your Wife and Son are very disturbed because you won't let them in the house. I told them to get out while I was working on a contract and I would be finished soon. The policeman went away and my Wife and Son came back into the house. Teresa pushed me over and tried to hit me. I defended myself by squirting her with some pop. I did not strike her. She cut her hand and said I attacked her. They both went away very upset. What they did next would anger any husband. Their excuse was, we thought you were sick. 2 policeman came to the door from Putnam County. Apparently, my Wife and Son between them had called the Baker Act on me. They were putting me. The only member of the family with any brains into an institution. They called it a C.S.U. facility. And only my wife could get me out. She firmly believed there was something wrong with me. At that time I thought I was fine. They didn't think of calling a Doctor. Getting back to the story, Good cop bad cop, what a bully 6ft tall, crew cut, 300lbs. Busting out of his uniform. You know the type, with muscles like a wrestler. I knew I was in for trouble, I had heard about American cops in some of these poky towns. I had never in my life had a conflict with the Police. No arrests ever. Green Card holder with legal status. The arsole cop said to me. Any guns in the house, will the 2 German shepards be okay. They were just sitting watching. I am glad, because knowing his mentality he would have shot them both. We both love these animals so much. These policemen came into my house uninvited. I wasn't hurting anybody. I am still an English citizen and my house is my castle and this would never happen. I chose to live here, so I must abide by American laws. This incident would never have happened in Palm Beach where the cops are more civilized. It takes all sorts I know and there are good and bad all over the world. During my stay in the nut house, a total of 3 weeks. I spoke to everyone that came through the doors. You see, even when I am in the wrong place I still talk to everybody to see what is going on. Most of them had drug problems and suicides and I was soon playing cards with the staff. The beds were terrible and I couldn't sleep. They had night guards on duty. One guy I used to call Hitler. One night because I would not stay in my room, he would drag me by the neck back to the room. I wouldn't give up. He had to in the end. Back to the forced entry into the house by the 2 policemen. Me to the cops. The guns are secure. Bully cop, We are here to arrest you under the Baker Act and to take you to a Hospital. Are you coming willingly or unwillingly. I didn't want to leave my house so like a twit I said unwillingly, but I wasn't about to resist or fight anybody. I was 75 years old with bad knees and unable to walk and also painful I shut the pain out of my mind. There was of course the nice cop, but you know how they stick together. After I said unwillingly all hell broke loose. Bully cop. Handcuffed my hands behind my back and forced me to the ground. Punched me in the ribs, I never knew such pain which lasted for 3 weeks. Threatened to tazor me and had it pressed to my neck. I wasn't resisting or going anywhere. He was just enjoying himself. I said I have bad legs and you are causing me terrible pain. He was treating me like a murderer. If he had used his tazor, I am sure it would have hurt, but I can stand pain. The other cop said, he didn't have to treat you so rough. You wasn't giving us any trouble. The next thing I was dragged to a police car and dumped in the back seat like a sack of potatoes. If I am just a medical case, why treat me so rough, I didn't harm anybody. I was shitting bricks, no wonder I was having a nervous breakdown (I thought at the time). All the neighbors were watching as they dragged me out I must have been the talk of the town. Fire truck, ambulance, All having a good laugh at my expense. I had to wait in a hot car for 30 min while the cop was bullshitting with the other guys They should have brought some food and had a party. I was dying of thirst. Finally the good cop decides to take me away. He was driving like a maniac. Didn't know where he was going, got lost a dozen times over a 30 mile journey. I said take it easy, get me there in one piece. His driving was the worst. If he wasn't a cop he would have been pulled over. We finally arrived at C.S.U. Meridian Group Gainesville. I was so dry by this time and I couldn't get a drink. I said I can't get out of this car I said. I was just in so much pain. A slim 100lb girl said to me, come with me to be evaluated, I still could not move and she had to pull me out. So they put me in the waiting room and gave me that glass of water, thank God. I think I would have died of thirst if I had to wait much longer. Then they took me to Shands Hospital for tests. X-rays on my ribs. I swore that I must have a dozen broken ribs because of the pain.

19

The bastard knew how to cause pain without breaking anything. They gave me all the tests including a brain scan and could uot find anything wrong with me. With the pain in the ribs, I could not sleep for weeks. Never had pain like it all my life. Always been healthy, I didn't start having trouble with my knees until I was 70. The bed was so uncomfortable in the hospital. Took ages to get water, not used to hospitals. Glad I am only staying one night By the way I got a bill for $445 for ambulance and Fire Truck. I didn't see any fires and I traveled in a police car and as for the hospital bill. I am sorry but I didn't have any insurance and I was forced into the situation anyway. I only had a couple of operations, the worst being the one for piles or hemorrhoids. I had this operation before coming to America They used to cut them out in the late 70s Can you imagine the pain afterwards. When I went to the toilet I had to sit in a hot bath afterwards for 15 mins to ease the pain. I did have another operation, it was a vasectomy. The other operation being the face lift. I never had any more trouble with the piles. I can remember my first visit to the Doctor's office. It was a super plush office with white carpet and I walked in out of the snow with shoes with deep grooves in, which left a tread of dirty snow all over the carpet. I wonder what the Doctor (we call them surgeons when they cut) thought. He probably put the price up. I was insured in those days and getting private rooms if I needed an operation. National Health was too slow. Insurance was cheap so it was well worth it. We live in Hawthorne and we have a Doctor there and my wife and I have waited as long as 4 hours in the Doctors office, and now it costs a hundred bucks to walk through the door. Talk about disorganization, or is it greedy grabbing Doctors trying to get rich off the poor in the country towns.Your guess is as good as mine but a lot of people can't afford to go to the Doctor's anymore and have to buy pain pills wherever they can. When I left Shands Hospital on 25th May the story becomes a series of thoughts and it is at this time I cannot remember everything that happened on this day, I remember going to the Nut House, but before arriving I had an attorney to represent me on the Court hearing, a pretty blonde girl from the State Attorney's office. She was my defender (I think) She could not have been any good as I got 30 days and my wife could extend to 90 days. That was in the facility to evaluate me. I can't remember any of this. Thanks Teresa and Clive, but I know you had my interests at heart and I guess there was something wrong with me. After arriving at C.S.U. I remember being questioned by the quacks and some other officials. They pumped all sorts of injections into me. I was definitely having some malfunction of the brain because everything was in the twilight zone. Which lasted a couple of days until they started feeding me drugs. Trouble is they were over medicating me and I was feeling like a zombie. They just could not get it right. If anyone had been through what I went through I am sure they would need medication too. I could not get out until my wife thought I was okay. Can you imagine what power that gave her. I looked after her for 25 years. Treated her like a queen, always putting her first. I could not afford health insurance for myself: but always looked after her. Paid it out of my pension. She bought a lot of champagne for herself, but I did not care. I loved her and I am not going to try and change her, It might ruin a good relationship. She had far more good qualities which many people do not have.

20

The shrink examined me, but said nothing. He was one of those guys with shifty eyes that could never look right at you. I called him Doctor Fu Man Chu. There was one thing I learnt while I was in this institution that you have to suck up to these guys or you will never get out. I should have learnt it sooner. He must have found something wrong with me, but he didn't tell me. I found out from my wife later that I had Bipolar A brain malfunction that was treatable with drugs, but one was committed to these drugs for life. Of course I had never heard of it before. So it was easy to pass me off with this condition. I didn't believe a word of it. On reading about it, there were so many famous people, past and present that had Bipolar Even Winston Churchill. They didn't know what they were doing at this place. 3 weeks and they still could not get the doses right. The beds were hard, the food was awful. I could not sleep and I couldn't go poop and I had a job to get laxatives from the nurse. I had never taken drugs in my life and this stupid Doctor did not know what he was doing. Some of the staff were very good and I used to play cards with them, but there were one or two that just had to be nasty. One of the patients reported a member of the staff to the hotline complaint dept. about me. A representative came round to see me after I had left the place. He said that he had heard that someone had been nasty to me and he wanted a name. I said that I could not remember and left it at that. During my 3 week stay I talked to most of the inmates to get their stories. Most of them had stories to tell about police brutalities and use of taser guns and how they love to use them. One guy said that he was drunk and had passed out on his bed at home, He had cut his wrist(not too deeply) Someone, Baker acted him while he was sleeping. Cops came in From Levie County with a dog that bit him on the leg. He offered no resistance and the cop tasered him and handcuffed him and the man was still passed out. Now I know there are two sides to every story. But I have heard so many tales, some of them must be true. This place was so disorganized it was a joke. Most of the staff were playing cards 90% of the time. They were not looking after us that is for sure. One of the bullies shouted at me at breakfast. He was a pig and one of the young inmates stuck up for me. He said, there was no need to talk to Mr. Watson like that. He was told to leave the room. He was a young guy with a few problems, but was not taking any shit from anybody. Go Dan go, somewhere in Gainesville. Hope we meet again sometime. We did actually meet again. I tried to help set him straight like I did with most people. He just needed some medication to calm him down. The staff were not much help. All they wanted to do was goof off. Temporary staff was a joke, these big old black girls about 350 lbs. Would come in and sit on a chair and never move and get $20 an hour, because temps get better pay than the regular staff. I offered to put in an exercise section and pay for it myself providing they would pay Teresa to oversee the project. There was nothing for the patients to do only watch T.V. They were too tight with their money too except my deal. And I never got a reply. After my 3 weeks stay at the luxury hotel, my wife decided after conferring with the Doctor that I could go home. For my continued supply of medication I was referred to Putnam Behavioral Healthcare. Julia Weber was the Nurse. She talked to me for 15 mins and said, you have Bipolar. She gave me the prescriptions. It was for the same stuff that I had been taking. I threw it in the trash, do not want to become a walking zombie thanks. I do not have Bi Polar anyway and I am feeling great. I did not keep my next appointment with Julia. Now my wife and I are going on a nice cruise to the Eastern Caribbean. I have forgiven her for what she did to me. She did not know any better. We were going to some great places St. Thomas, St. Marten and other Islands that we had seen before. The ship was the Carnival Valor. Perhaps Teresa will get back to normal on the trip, as she has changed. Keeps telling me to take my medication and I know I do not need it.

21

We are going away the 3rd July to the 10th of July , leaving Miami at 5pm Sunday. A beautiful ship, but chocker block full. Never again on a holiday week. Most expensive time too and too many kids. I am not saying the ship was bad. The entertainment and food was good. Cabins and facilities were good. More for the young people. The cruise was a disaster as far as our relationship goes. My Wife kept on at me to take my medicine, and I kept telling her that it made me feel like a zombie and I wasn't going to take it. Her personality seemed to have changed and I did not like it. She had always been such a sweet person. But she was getting on my nerves. She said, if you don't take your medicine your brain will explode. Perhaps she will get back to normal, she has been a changed woman since my discharge from C.S.U. still thinks I have Bipolar and does not like the new me. At the shows I would go up close so that I could see what was going on better, the shows were great. She would sit at the back to be awkward. I would walk out and leave her at the end of the show. One time we were together, she walked out of the show because she did not like it. However the following act was a hypnotist, and he was the best I have ever seen. He had 18 out of 20 completely hypnotized. One person would stand up every 15 seconds and shout I love you. Another girl was chasing a toy rabbit. All sorts of strange things were going on. Everybody was laughing, I really had a good time. It was a pity Teresa missed it, I know she would have enjoyed it. At the Ports she was walking 50 feet in front of me. I was trying to take some pictures and she was just being awkward and walking along as if she wasn't with me. I could see that our marriage was sinking fast. She wanted to make all the decisions since I went into the C.S.U. and I was not having that. She had the power to put me away and there was nothing I could do about it. We spent most of the cruise dodging each other. It was then I decided to write a book of my life in America I have had such a full life and perhaps people could learn from my mistakes. They might even save money. I took a lot of pictures and we were actually smiling on some of them, so we must have had some happy times. Another thing that pissed me off. We were in one of the ports and heading back to the ship. There was a bus coming so I got on the bus. Teresa wanted to walk and at that time my legs were bone on bone on the knee joints and it was hurting me. I had a push walker to help me and no one would help me onto the bus so I was really struggling. In the end a young teenager helped me. Teresa did not care, she was gone. she just kept walking. We had a good time in St.Thomas I bought 15 bottles of booze for $100 and they were delivered to the ship, for us to pick up when we arrived back in Miami. We bought our own perfume, and I bought Teresa a beautiful bracelet for her birthday which was only 2 weeks away. We have known St. Thomas for more than 20 years and still think it is one of the best Ports In the Eastern Caribbean except for St.Martin, wbich is a little cheaper so it has got to be number 1. We get everything we want shopping on the main street and then we hang out on the nice little beach adjacent to the main street. One has to take a shuttle boat from the ship. It costs $5 return and you can go back and forth as many times as you like at no extra charge. We had a nice afternoon in the sun, lounging in our deck chairs under a sun shade. I do not drink, but I went crazy and drank 4 margarita and didn't even get a buzz. Time to go back to the ship, it would be terrible to miss the ship, so we always get back at least an hour before sailing. We never buy any food in any of the ports. They feed you so much on the ship for free. Why would you want to pay for it. Some people still do. We had our good times and I still loved Teresa but I was going to get a divorce. Being married gave her too much power. I still want to stay with her, but she probably won't go for that. So we will have to see what happens. We had great service on the ship. On the first day I tipped everybody, even the Head waiter. She said, what did you do that for. I said, we are celebrating our anniversary and we will get the best of everything. They will treat us like Royalty. Its just not like you she said. I was the owner of 2 large restaurants in England and I knew how they all looked forward to getting their tips. These guys work hard on the ship. The cruise lines work them hard all hours of the day and night. Most of the staff have to send all their money home to support their families. They have to learn our language before they can get a job. Just a limited amount to allow them to converse with the passengers. They are mostly from the far east, most likely from somewhere you have never heard of You will not find an American working on the Cruise Ships. You will find Brits working in the casinos, I do not know why. Everyone is polite and willing to help.

22

Tipping paid off, they would bring us 2 main course dishes and we would pick out the best and put it together and leave the fattening stuff. We don't even put on weight on a cruise anymore. We just watch what we eat. No fun getting fat and bloated and putting on another 15lbs like we used to on our early cruising days. I used to starve myself before a cruise and after I had to go on a diet for 3 months. I kept on asking Teresa to have a drink. The more I asked the more she said no. I have been using the wrong system all these years this turned out to be the worst vacation we have ever had. Since 1982 we have been so close and now things are not the same. I can't remember in all the years we were together us having a real argument. We were soulmates. Always enjoying one anothers company. We did everything together. I knew she still loved me, but she done something to me which should never have happened. We accepted each other for our little differences. If she wanted to drink, it was okay. I am not her mother. She probably didn't like some of the things I did. There was no other woman for me. We arrived at Miami on Sunday morning to utter chaos. Two ships Valor & Victory, both Carnival ships. About 10,000 people trying to get off the ships in a 300ft front area. My Son Clive was picking us up. He probably had to circle the area 10 times before we could get through customs. He brought us down and was picking us up, a total distance 260mls for the 2 trips. I gave him $20 to cover the gas. You should have seen his face, I know he expected more. They made a day of it, so it was a day out for him and his Cuban girl friend after they had dropped us off. Anyway he picked us up (I never knew he was such a bad driver, Teresa will confirm) he was all over the road. On the way down he got lost even with his G.P.S. and blamed us all for talking. What a spoiled brat. Am I really to blame. I did my best bringing him up. Teresa and I were staying with Clive and his Cuban bitch (God help him if he marries her) But he is so in love. It is only a matter of time. Hope he gets her to sign a pre nuptural but I do not think he will. She will take him to the cleaners before he knows what day it is. He has learnt nothing from me. He does have some good points. Doesn't drink or smoke or do drugs and no trouble with the police. He is a good person but doesn't have his priorities right. He sings the same old tune. Dad has never loved me. He put me in a foster-home; But it was only for a short time while I was getting a home and business ready. All the bad things I had done to Clive. All this was blurted out by his girl friend, no not blurted, but shouted. Of course he never told her the good things I had done for him. Then I told them I was divorcing Teresa. I have never known such a mouthful from the Cuban bitch. She was shouting at me as if I was a child and Clive and Teresa said nothing. I was insulted in my Son's house by his live in girlfriend. I was on my way out the door. I didn't have to stay there. It was only for one night anyway. Teresa said, calm down we will get up early and be gone before they wake up. The night before she cooked a meal for us, it was so bad, we thought we were going to choke, But Clive loved her cooking so much. He must have hated mine all the years I looked after him on my own. Of course I said the food was wonderful, I didn't want to hurt her feelings. That was before she started shouting at me. Up to then she had been so nice and polite. Teresa said that it was my BiPolar that was causing all the problems. BiPolar my arse I said. We left next morning very early and said goodbye to Clive. I said that I never wanted to speak or see him again. I told Teresa that I didn't want him at my funeral. He was history and I meant it. Lets go back a day. I had made an appointment with Edyth for lunch as a surprise. She was her old boss at the Beauty shop. Because of our situation she didn't want to go. I said I will go on my own then., Suit yourself. We arrived for lunch at 1:30pm on Sunday. It was my intension to move back to Palm Beach and get Teresa her old job back. I suggested $500 per week plus 1% of the gross takings of the shop. They laughed at me. I told them that they didn't know how to run a business. Poor George the husband, a retired cop had no say. He stayed at home, he was on a good pension. Edyth who was getting on in years was the top producer in the shop. Had to keep working to support her son who also worked in the shop. Through his rudeness to clients had lost a lot of customers over the years. I said, now is the time to sell your Ocean Front Condo and move inland and buy some acreage so you do not have to pay all the fees which keep going up. George was in agreement, but Edyth will stay until she dies. They would have room for their Son's horses too. I told George that Teresa had Baker Acted me. He said, how could you have done that to your husband. For the next 4 hours he was on my side. I told him I was going to divorce Teresa. Ken he says, you are making a big mistake. She will get another man so easy because she is so pretty. George doesn't know me. It will be just like starting another chapter of my life again, I did it all the time in England. Teresa knows what I am like. I could not eat now as the conversation was getting really hot. I drank only a little of the red wine to be sociable. Edyth was sticking up for Teresa and she had always said during her 2 years absence from the beauty shop, please come back.

23

Teresa we miss you so much. Course they did they lost most of their customers while she was away. I told Edyth that if she had paid Teresa what she was worth I would have stayed in Palm Beach and Teresa would still be working at Posh For Hair. George pipes up, I didn't know she was not getting paid enough. (Wake up and smell the roses George) What will happen when Edyth can't work I dread the moment. It appears now, that the business is so bad, they can't afford to give Teresa her job back. So we left the penthouse and intended to go back to my Son's house. Teresa gets into the car and says, you are sick and can't drive. I called 911 I wasn't taking any bullshit from anyone. Within 5 minutes the chief of police and 3 cop cars arrived. Sir said the chief of police. What is the problem. My wife is in the driving seat and won't let me drive my car. We are going in for a divorce and she is being awkward. Sir I have been in the same situation as you, but as your wife, she can drive your car and you can't do a thing about it while you are married. If you don't stop the fussing I will clap you both in jail as you are both living in a County away from here. The chief said that I could drive the car. Another cop came up to the chief and said Mrs. Watson is driving the car. The chief looked amazed, but said okay. I found out later that she had told the cop that I had 2 glasses of wine and I was on medication. How easy she lies. I had less than half a glass of wine and my pain pills do not affect my driving. She wouldn't let me drive back to North Florida. We usually do half each. I don't care, she is a good driver. Almost as good as me. I think I would handle an emergency situation better if it ever came about. I tend to drive faster and will overtake when necessary. The following day I went into the

Real Estate office in Melrose and told the Broker that I was moving back to Palm Beach. I had an offer to join my old broker. She was getting a new building and expanding her business and incorporating a mortgage company. I called Teresa from the office and told her that I was going to Palm Beach. She said, you are not going. That was it, I put the phone down on her and would not except any calls from her. I asked the broker to try and get the house that we had sold, closed as soon as possible. I stayed in Gainesville for about 3 days and then went over to say goodbye to Annette who was Teresa's sister who lived in Okechobee. Then on to a hotel in West Palm. I did not have a lot of money as our money was tied up in the house. Teresa had the credit cards and the one I was using. she stopped. I cashed out a bank account which was only a little over $1,000 but I couldn't use it for 10 days. I spent a whole night shopping in Walmart while I was in Gainesville. One can buy a complete wardrobe with all the toiletries, razor and 4 nice cases for very little money. I stayed at the Red Roof Inn and parked the car in a very illuminated location. The car was only 3 months old and I didn't want it trashed. I was getting very concerned about the closing and the broker was ignoring me, so I faxed over Some nasty letters to get his arse in gear, which did not help. Everyone was lying. The buyer couldn't get insurance because there were hurricanes out there, which sounded reasonable. I didn't trust my broker, he has very shifty eyes. He could never look me in the eyes. He was making a fortune but I think he was expanding too fast He would be away from his Melrose office for days and never leave anyone in charge to make decision. The property should have closed July 12th 2005. Teresa and I had left the property in the brokers hands to have the closing ready for when we came back off the cruise. I called the bank to see what was going on, they said the broker had been very lax. He had recommended an appraiser that never showed up and had delayed everything. I was mad because the broker had lied to me. I went to see Bill Gordon the closing Attorney(should be selling fruit at Waldo Flea Market) I told him that my wife and I were getting a divorce and I did not want to be at the closing at the same time as my wife. I left her cell phone and asked him if he would give it to her. He was so scared of me I think he nearly shit himself. Everyone was beginning to think I was crazy. I was going off at everybody. I was sick about the whole thing. After checking out Palm Beach, I decided that it was not for me it was too busy. I called the bank that was doing the loan. They said that Bill Gordon was refusing to do the closing and I had better get back, otherwise it is never going to close. Meanwhile, Teresa had already let the buyer move in on the 23 July and we did not have a closing date. I was furious, You just don't do that You have to see the money first She is a nice person just gone through a divorce and she has to have a place for her son and horses, so says Teresa.

24

In the end I had to agree. She had just gone through a divorce and needed a place for her horses. At the present time she had been leasing and the place was unsuitable, and we could have lost her. I went back on Thursday 28th July expecting to close on the 29th. I had no money and nowhere to live so I went back to my home. I said to Teresa on the phone that I was taking one of the dogs. That did it, I should not have opened my big mouth. She got herself an attorney who blocked the sale of the property. I had negotiated a heavy duty truck while I was in Palm Beach. I wanted it to pull a 45 foot 5th wheel which I was going to live in on a campsite, about 50 miles away from our home. I was going to write my book and do Real Estate. She would not release any funds so I had to scrap the idea. We had already ordered a 29 foot camper that we could pull with our van. Teresa was in a right state when I arrived at the house. The gate was locked and the front and back doors were locked and she would not let me in. I had to reason with her. I said I have no money and nowhere to go. She would not let me in. I had to call 911. I knew that I was entitled to enter my own house according to Florida Law. The police were there for over an hour, man and woman cops. At that moment I really hated myself, seeing Teresa in tears, broke my heart. I still loved her very much. I just didn't no what was happening to us. Eventually she gave in and the police went away after asking a friend in the area to stay the night to ensure peace between us. There was no trouble, I would never hurt her, I still loved her after all. I stayed in the house and we got on okay. We closed on the property on the 9th of August after getting another Title co. to do the closing. Gordon thought I was incompetent to sign. Who the hell is he to make those decisions. Someone wanted me to get a note from my Doctor to say that I was of sound mind. I told them to take a running jump off a short plank. I didn't have to prove anything. A day before the closing, the bank decided that the buyer didn't have enough money to pay the closing costs. I had to up the price $5,000 and pay it back to the buyers. It is a good job the property appraised for the extra. I went and picked up the 29 foot camper we ordered. We had a $2,000 deposit on it that we were about to lose. I told Teresa of my plan about moving away about 50 miles to write my book. I needed time on my own, no woman would ever control my life again: Teresa did not want a divorce. I would always love her and we could still live together, but we would not be married anymore. I said that I would fix up the property and do all the jobs in the yard and leave in October. I filed for divorce with an attorney in Palatka and paid all the money up front. I told Teresa that their was no one else and I would always love her. I just could not let anyone have the power to put me away again, and I could not get out without a release from her. I worked hard in the yard, I prepared the driveways and footpath and areas that needed to be concreted and then got a couple of guys to spread the concrete. They were supposed to be specialist. They made a right mess, and they didn't put in the expansion joints and now we have a lot of cracks. I also built a nice porch off the front door. I had so much energy, I couldn't understand where it was coming from. I was nasty to Teresa, she seemed to have changed, but looking back it was all my fault. We took our camper to a beautiful campground in Jacksonville, it was right on the beach. It was August and the weather was fantastic. We had our 2 German Shepards, Duchess and Lady with us. I loved those dogs so much. The only trouble was, Teresa had to get up and take the dogs for a walk every morning and last thing at night. I couldn't walk the distance at that time. It was then I realized I was being such a fool. We were laying in bed and I looked down at her sweet face and I could see the pain I had caused her. I said I am cancelling the divorce and I am going to stay with you. I was still not taking my medication. As far as I was concerned, There was nothing wrong with me. We had a great time and I am sure the dogs had a good time. After our vacation I was different. I was calling Teresa nasty names and I know she was getting sick of it. I didn't know why I was doing this. It was completely out of character for me. I try to be a nice person, if I can to everybody, yet I am being nasty to the person I love. There is something wrong somewhere. Amongst all this confusion I had time to order a new car for me. Teresa was getting fed up with all the mental abuse, so she said that she was going down to Annettes for an undetermined time. Okay I said, but drop me off in Ocala so that I can pick up my new car. So that is what she did and no goodbye kiss. The car was not ready, so they gave me a loner and I picked it up about a week later. Teresa came back 8 days later and I told her that she was going to have her old husband back and there was going to be no more nastiness between us. And everything was alright again. The house was looking nice, all the concrete work was done and we had a nice pad for the camper. We went to the same campground again to celebrate Thanksgiving and we had a good time, just like old times, We had the dogs with us and they had a good time. They love Teresa so much. I am just an afterthought but they have always been nice to me and never growled or bit me. Then came Christmas and all Teresas' family came to spend it with us. I like it when they come, I am sure Teresa gets sick of my face and she does like company. Then comes the New Year' Eve. We always stay home and have the same meal. Lobster tail Fillet Mignon Baked Potato, Asparagus and Peas. We don't want to mix it with the drunken drivers. Now it is 2006, how time flies. Teresa's sister Linda wants to sell her house and she has been unsuccessful with the local brokers.

25

We decided to kill two birds with one stone. Go to West Palm in our camper and stay at the Safari grounds where you get free admission to the Safari. The campgrounds were good too. We took Teresa's Aunt Lowes with us and she always has a good time with us. I think she was about 82 at that time. Then we went to see Linda's house, actually half of the house belonged to Wally, the man she had lived with for about 35 years, divorced for a long time but still living with him, But now wants to sell up and get her own place. I convinced them that I could sell the properly. I signed them up on a listing agreement and I put my license with a local broker and within 2 months I had sold it. Teresa and I went down to the closing as we were expecting trouble from Wally. Sure enough he opened his big mouth and said He wanted $40,000 more than Linda because that was what she had agreed to. Teresa tried to reason with him and he called her some nasty names. Linda gave in, she just wanted to get away from the man. I put a clause in the contract, saying he had to move all the junk off the properly within 30 or 40 days. I can't remember exactly. He said no problem, but he sat on his arse most of the time and lost $20,000. There was a lot of junk. Trucks, boats, cars, 48 foot trailers. You name it it was there. The price of property was high at this time and we had to locate Linda into something. All she could afford was a cheap mobile home in a Trailer Park. It was a nice Park with a Lake and she loved the mobile home. It was also close to work and she would save on gas and time. We decided that camping Was not for us. It was too much work. We had been used to cruises and being waited on. We put the camper up for sale. I couldn't afford the payment on the car and so I took it back to the dealers. It Was July and I decided that I was going to get some estimates to get my knees done. I had suffered long enough. The Doctor wanted $3,000 the Hospital wanted $15,000, Figure $3,000 for the Anesthesiologist. Did not get an estimate. Then it was $45 per hour for therapy Almost $22,000. Not bad when the insurance get a bill for about $130,000 according to another person I talked to that was having it done through his insurance company. Both my legs turned out good because I had a great Doctor and I am sure that God Was guiding his hand. His name is Doctor David Risch and has such a nice personality every time you see him he has a smiling face. My advice to anyone contemplating knee surgery is to have them done both together. The pain is really bad first day after the operation, but now I can walk good, my legs are straight and there is no pain. It was about 3 months after having my knees done, there was a change coming over me. I told the broker that she didn't know what the hell she Was doing. That part was really true. This was all over the phone, She fired me on the phone and sent the police round to make sure I didn't steal anything. She had about $100 of junk. No one worked there only me. I was trying to get a new branch office open for her. Nobody else would work for her. She screwed me out of some of my commission too. Thank you Linda Freund of Palm Beach County, but no hard feelings what goes around comes around and as you are such a lousy sales person. I bet you are not doing too good right now. I went into Walmart in Palatka and noticed in the parking lot that 2 of the handicap spaces were completely full of shopping carts. I took photographs, as I had a handicap sticker because of my knees, Then I asked to see the manager to make her aware of what Was going on. She completely ignored me. I was doing some shopping while I was waiting for her. I must have waited at least an hour before a cop from the narcotics section approached me and said, Sir I have been asked to escort you off the premises and please leave your proposed purchases behind. Now why did that happen. Something must have scared the manager. If I had reported her to head office and mentioned about the handicap spaces being blocked, she would probably have been fired. It is always customer first at Walmart. Then there was another situation shortly after. An Auction was advertised. It Was a Lake Front properly on Hampton Lake, it was a very desirable properly and I was going to bid on it. Unfortunately I got locked out of my vehicle and had to call a locksmith. I was going to be a few minutes late so I called them. I arrived 5 minutes late and the auction was all over. I asked to see whoever was in charge, but the owner was hiding. Now I am an Auctioneer and I have never done an auction on an important properly in less than half an hour. Usually it is at least an hour. Another thing which I thought was strange. Within an hour after the auction, heavy machinery arrived to demolish the house that was unliveable. To me, that meant that the buyer had already been decided before the auction. I was going to report it, but I let it go. Now we have to go for a repeat of what happened when I again locked Teresa out of the house.

26

First of all, my family came over from England in August. Just after I had my knees done. It is always a pleasure to see them. We had just had an ahove ground swimming pool installed. Which is a lot of fun, and I went crazy, exercising my legs. I cut down my therapy time by more than half. In doing so I injured a tendon in my left ankle and it was painful to walk. The Doctor put a boot on me and told me to be careful. So that was the end of my swimming for now. It was the other leg that I snapped my Achilles tendon in the nineties. So when it healed it became stronger. I always have to find jobs for Roy, he can't sit still for 5 minutes. The more he sits the more he smokes. I can't make him stop. Just like my mother and father, all they did was smoke when they were sitting at home. My brother and I never smoked. I think my family from England like coming over to see us. Teresa makes them very welcome. Yvon just asked me if they could come over every year instead of every other year. Of course I said yes, our place must be better than a Hotel. It is a pity that my other daughter Linda cannot find it in her heart to forgive me. Getting back to when I locked Teresa out of the house again. I told her that I was working under cover for the Real Estate Commission and not to come in the office as I had a lot of papers that I was working on that she could not see. Looking back, I know what she must have been thinking. He is talking crazy again. Then she took the dogs and stayed in a Hotel for 3 days. She came back with her sister Annette and a friend as if nothing had happened. Teresa prepared a nice steak dinner and everything was fine. I thought Teresa was intoxicated the way she was acting, but her sister said she had not been drinking. The following day, they were all outside and I locked the door to stop them coming back in. I told them that I had papers that I did not want them to see. Teresa called the cops again. Just my luck again, Here comes this big 350lb bully. I know he wants to tear me to pieces by the look on his face. If you don't open the door, I will smash it down. Of course I open the door. Bear in mind I never laid a finger on my wife. He handcuffed me and dumped me in his car like a sack of potatoes. I didn't even know what I was being charged with. He really hurt my legs and he drove like a maniac, stopping and jerking the car to give me as much pain as he could. This time I was taken straight to jail, do not pass go, do not collect $200. I had never in my life been to jail. All I saw was a bunch of low lifes awaiting distribution. The place was like a Gestapo Headquarters. I have never seen anything like it in all my life. I didn't belong there. My only crime was to lock out my Wife. I ask you, is that an offence that requires jail. I was never charged with anything, so I presume that I still have a clean record. Who knows and who cares any way. I was offered a meal at the time they put me in the cell and I refused it, I wish I hadn't because it looked pretty good. You should have seen the cell. Dirty old stainless steel potty, which one would hate to have a crap on. Single bed with no mattress and a dirty old floor. I was right next to a crazy person and all he could do was to dump water all over me every few minutes. I started throwing it back thinking he might stop. I had to suffer this for 3 days. I was so wet, I never got any sleep at all. I had heard things about American jails in some of these hick towns. They wanted me out of the cell so they could clean. I said I am not moving until I get a note from the British Consul. I really thought they were going to kill me.I was expecting the F.BI. To come and rescue me. I still did not know that there was something wrong with me. It took 3 guys to drag me out of the cell but I did get a note from the British Consul so I felt okay. There was also a note for me to appear before the judge. So they handcuffed me and put leg irons on me and transported me with a bunch of hooligans to see the judge. Teresa and Annette were watching me struggling along with my bad legs and leg irons. I don't think they were enjoying the scene. The judge said I needed to go for an evaluation. I was then transported to the CSU at Lake City. This proved to be a much nicer place than the one at Gainesville. There were no dictators or bullies. I took an instant dislike to the Doctor. She saw me for 5 minutes and said that I had Bipolar. I said to myself she is the crazy one if she thinks that I have Bipolar. I made a big mistake again, I should have sucked up to her and kissed her arse. Oh but was she ugly, if she smiled her face would crack. They put me on the Bipolar medication and I had no problems with it. Not like the Gainesville branch who made me feel like a zombie after taking the medication. There was very little to do here, we had lots of talks and pencil and paper questions, but that was no fun. At Gainesville there was more to entertain us. Arts and crafts and different types of games and a nice person in charge of that section to cheer you up if you were down. Then comes the day of my evaluation, I get a defense Attorney on my side. How lucky can you get and I don't have to pay, and I don't have to pay for my stays in the C.S.U.s Either. The Attorney was worse than useless and everybody said that I needed treatment for Bipolar. There was one incident when I think they over medicated me. They nearly killed me at Lake City. They had to rush me to the hospital. After a bunch of tests they shipped me back as good as new. I was there for 3 weeks, They transported me home which was about 90 miles. I was so happy to see Teresa, she had lost a lot of weight and looked really good. She always looks good. Just as pretty as the day I met her.

27

It was after my stay that I finally realized that I had Bipolar and would have to continue with my medication to avoid getting manhandled by the police and dumped into the nut house again. Only 2 lithium tablets per day and $4 to Walmart per month. You can't beat that. I think I have this malfunction for life, but with medication I seem quite normal and feel great. Strange that I should get it so late in life. I bad so much energy when I was off the medication, but Teresa couldn't stand me and I had to keep her happy or she might turn me in again and I wouldn't like that. She is the love of my life. It is 18 months since I was in the C.S.U. Things have been pretty quiet. The Real Estate market is really bad and the economy is terrible. I think the president has done a bad job and I am glad we will be getting a new one soon. It is now the middle of 2008 and time is flying. Our combined life insurance has gone up from under $1,500 per year to over $9,000 and that was only for $100,000 We can't afford that, so we will have to let it go. It is a real shame as I have covered Teresa for decades. Teresa is working part time at C.S.U Pharmacy but if she can get a better job she will. She would like something interesting, But her qualifications are not too numerous. Thanks to her father for dragging her out of school to early. I had to get a blood test last week for a Lithium level. The Doctor has to monitor this to protect ones kidneys. I kept putting it off and he said if you don't get it done I will have to take you off Lithium. Now Lithium was only $4 for a month's supply at Walmart and the other drug he was talking about was more than 10 times that amount. I hurried down to the Hospital to get the test. To my surprise it had gone up from $42 to $143. So I went elsewhere to cut my costs in half I don't. know who sets the prices in Hospitals. When I got a price for my knees, they added another $1,000 when I went to pay. And they wanted all the money up front. Then I needed a couple more days and I paid up front for the stay. I got another bill over $3,000 in the mail. Of course they never got it and cancelled it when I complained. I don't know their situation, but it seems like Hospitals are just after as much money as they can get out of you. Our last vacation was in November of 2007 and we cruised the Eastern and Western Caribbean. The port was in Miami. First of all we had to drop the dogs off in Ocala for 17 days. Juliet our cat traveled with us to Teresa's sister Linda who was going to look after the cat. We stayed overnight and went to the port by train and taxi. I don't know how much we saved on parking fees but I am sure it was up to $15 a day for parking at the port. The train fare from Linda's was very cheap, so we saved quite a bit over $100. We had a nice time, but it went so quick. and it must have cost us nearly $5,000 when you add in the boarding charges and all the other bits and pieces. As the old saying goes, you can't take it with you. It is always nice to come home, the worst job being the unpacking. Sorting out the mail too. 99% of which are bills. We had a nice meal with Linda before leaving at Red Lobster, not my favorite place. I would sooner eat Chinese. I think Linda wanted to keep the cat. I know she spoiled her. We can't seem to feed her enough and she always eats all of her meals. Before, she always left half.

28

I am almost finished with my story. I am 78 years old, but I tell people that I am 58 and they believe me. I am still vain and in good health. I am living with Teresa who is my wife and also the love of my life after 26 years of being together. I am not working at the moment as I am taking time out to write my book. I have a pension from England every month, which is about $700 per month, which is not enough to live on. I still have my license for Real Estate and I also have an Auctioneers License and I will soon be going back to work I look back and think, if I hadn't gone into the business ventures with other people. I would be very rich now. But what is rich, I have had a good full life and done everything I wanted. Who wants to go up in space anyway. So what if I am living in a mobile home right now. We have been here for 5 years and we normally move every 5 years so we don't have to decorate or renew the appliances. The thing is, I am playing the cards that I was dealt I have never gone out to hurt anyone. I forgive the people that screwed me out of my money. Teresa get my guns out the safe, I am going hunting. Some of them are probably dead by now. Houtris from the La Tava, who screwed me out of $80,000 and he died pretty young after closing the restaurant. I haven't checked on anybody else, I try not think about those terrible days when I was so stupid. I would never go into a partnership again and I am a lot more careful when giving money away. Although I live in America through choice, I never forget the country where I was borne, but everything is so expensive, I would have to be a millionaire again to move back. Life is very quiet here in Hawthorne. Nice countryside to retire to, but I am not ready to retire yet. There are no good paying jobs here, not like Palm Beach County. I went after 6 jobs for car sales man. They all advertised, no experience necessary. The

B.M.W. company wanted 10 salesmen as they were expanding. By law they are not supposed to ask your age. Guess what, they always want to see your driving license and then they know your age. Every week there is a dealer looking for car salesmen. I wonder why, the terms and wages seem great. Mazda wouldn't even give me a job delivering cars, and I have never had a claim on my insurance and I am classified as a good driver. I applied for several other jobs, but no luck. It would be nice if just one of the the people would send you a letter or a telephone call to let you know if you had been accepted or rejected. We fill in these complicated forms, and they want to know everything. Even Teresa at 50 had the same problems and had to settle for a job she doesn't like. In Palm Beach she managed a beauty shop and was paid well and she enjoyed going. Thanks Gainesville, at least I can always make money in Real Estate. I am glad I got that License in 1988. I made a mistake by moving about 275 miles north, I wonder when I am going to do something right. It had better be soon as I must be running out of time. The clock is ticking. To people in Europe that are thinking about moving to America. You need to buy a small or large business that is making money. See the tax returns before making a decision or parting with any money. Avoid partnerships, learn by my mistakes. If you don't know how to value a business, get help. I have helped several people over the years and know how to value a business. You may be very rich and you don't need a job or a business. Then you are very lucky and have come to the right country. If you are over 40 you are not likely to get a good job. You might even have to be under 30 for some jobs. The positives are, everything is a lot cheaper in America than Europe. Even gas is cheaper and of course the weather in Florida where we live is sunshine, nearly every day and you can buy big chunks of land very cheap. Whatever you do, I wish you luck.

29

2010

The British Consul called me when I was in the nut house. Not that he can do anything, but it was nice to get a cheerful voice. I wonder how they found out. If you are traveling within 30 miles of Gainesville, check out G.M, service department on Main Street. You will get the best service for 12.95 and it will be done right I had a quote from Chevrolet in Palatka for a brake job, it was $2,000. G,M, did it for $500. Dave the manager will not screw you, He should be the general manager and Ian the service manager. Mr President, the cops in America are bullies, there is no need for it, you can fix it. I can give you examples of their brutality. By the way, you are doing a good job with what you have to work with. I was named Rico suave by the staff at csu. I rather like that name, I think I will Keep it.

2009

It is June 2009 and a lot has happened this year. Teresa got a job as a C.NA, having passed all the necessary exams. She doesn't like the job. having been in the beauty business most of her life, it is a big change. But Gainesville is not Palm Beach and the money sucks and one has to travel 30 miles to a job, which also sucks, not to mention the wear and tear on the vehicle and the gas. As real estate was so bad I got a job selling water systems, but that didn't work out, so I gave it up. Teresa went to Lowes's funeral in North Carolina, she was her Mothers Sister. She was Teresa's favorite. Teresa was going through the change of life and I have had a hard time dealing with it. It all started in June 2009. Most people she talked to on the phone she finished off the conversation with, love you, but never to me. Her kisses were like grandma kisses. I said if that's the best you can do forget it. Then something happened that I never expected. She said I want to live on my own, We have nothing in common and you have lost all your drive. And you should be in an old folks home. Where you can be looked after. Mind you, she is the one that needs care she always has a pain somewhere and has to go to a chirpractor for adjustments ever other week. We have slept in separate beds since June. That must be a sign that our 29 year romance is coming to an end I still love Teresa ,but she always interferes in my business decisions. she will spend $10,000 doing up the kitchen ,but she will object to me spending, money to make money. We have our house up for sale right now, but it is priced to high and there is too much clutter. We sold a house at Stark, *it took us 3 years to sell, so that was the end. and we still made $12,000.*

2010

I am almost finished writing this book and I know you are going to enjoy reading it. Everything in the book is a true account of my life and I know you will learn something from It by the mistakes I made. I am not working at the moment. I am taking time to write this book so that others can benefit from the reading. I have a pension from England which is not enough to live on, but I can always supplement this by selling Real Estate or doing an Auction or selling a business, I am qualified to do all these things. If I hadn't been so stupid going into business with scam merchants I would still have a million bucks in the bank, But what is rich, I have had a good life and done everything I wanted, except one thing. I want the number 2 playboy mansion and I will have 7 beautiful girls and they will be called the Silent Seventh after the truckers seventh gear which is a coasting gear from the old days., I am playing the cards I was dealt I think God was the dealer. I have never gone out of my way to hurt anybody. I am Bipolar manic after all and I thank God for that, I can't stop talking and I am always trying to make people feel good. Some of the people that screwed me are probably dead by now. Houtris who owed me $80,000 IS dead. He was the one that bought La Tava back off me and made a mess of it and he lost it I should have kept it and it would still be a fabulous place. I live in America but I have to move out of Florida because of the Baker Act which is grossly misinterpreted and used with hatred, I am British but

I choose to live in America because of the weather and other opportunities that are not available in England, I am not a snob and I would speak to a hobo and show him the same respect as I would the president of the United States of America Not like some of the snobs in Keller Williams office in Florida and the wannabe manager that doesn't know what an exclusive agency is. She calls it a pocket listing. The broker would be better off sticking with her bar although she is clever the bar is more enticing as real estate is slow right now.

30

Could you believe anyone being so brutal to an 80 year old man. This
will be a surprise to the world, and he was doing no harm to anyone.
Police brutality, stuck in a hot police car with no water for 3 hours and
they would not give me a drink of water. I had some in the van. I had an
appointment with Teresa's boss. Comfort keepers. I should have listened
to Teresa, She didn't want me to interfear, she was quite happy doing slave
labour. Getting back to the story. *I* opened the van door and all hell
broke loose. 4 cops surrounded me with guns drawn. I think I must be
Ben Ladin and I must have an atom bomb in the van. They searched it
but it must have slipped through the floorboards. I did not resist arrest
they never cautioned me yet they smashed my head to the concrete, broke
my glasses, made my head and nose bleed painfully, There was about 6
cop cars enjoying the view. Is this America Mr. President; Or are we in
Afganistan. I thought we were supposed to be setting an example to the
rest of the world. We are baker acting you, one of the cops growled, like a
gestapo agent from many moons ago, Hitlers regime. Why would anyone
want to Baker Act me. I *was taking my medicine, there was nothing wrong
with me,* it was just the spiteful bitch acting out her P.Q. 's Remember lady,
paybacks are hell We finally arrived at the nut house at the Meridian and
much to my surprise they were wonderful people, so different from 5 years
ago. You were treated like a human being. I had to sleep on the floor the
first night , but that was okay, at least I had a mattress The second night was
okay, 2 beds to a room and up at 6a.m for vital signs and medicine. The
food was great. More food than one could eat. And seconds if required.
What a difference from the time I came before when the staff were. Like
little hitlers. The doctor said take your medicine and you would be able

to leave in 3 days. Then the black man said that he wanted me to stay for another couple of days. I said no way. He said he would have to put it before the court. That was it you can't fight city hall. So I stayed at the holiday camp after calling him an arsoll. I always meet a lot of nice people in the C.S.U and I try to help them as some of them are lost soles and their mind seems to to be floating in space. I am a Bipolar Manic and I am on a constant high all the time. I can charm the pants off 99 women out of a 100 if I feel so inclined. I have never had a nightmare and have never felt violent towards anybody. I always have to speak to everyone in any room or to people I pass in the street. If I get any pain, my brain tells the section involved that there is no pain. A typical example was the spurs on my heels. The xrays were there to prove it. They hurt like a bitch, and I put pads in my shoes to lessen the pain, Screw this, they don't hurt, and that was the end of the pain. I have always had the ability to pick up women, as I have no fear of rejection. One can't win all the time, but if you are rejected, then go on to the next one. One doesn't even have to be handsome. Just got to have the gift of the gab. Since becoming bipolar manic, my brain power has multiplied a thousand times and I can remember so many things. My brain is like a computer but it cannot store names or faces. In fact I feel that God is working through my brain to keep my body free of disease. Bill Gates doesn't have enough money to buy my brain. (not that he would want to).

31

After my spell at C.S.U I decided to visit my son and his girl friend at West Palm Beach. We never have got on well together, but I thought it was time to change all that. After all none of us are getting any younger especially me. Clive sells cars over the intemet. Like any other business , times were tough, and with all his mortgage payments he is struggling. Aren't we all. His little boy D.J is a great kid and Clives Girl friend, Bobby Joe is the nicest person one could ever meet. I showed her how to cook ribs. I told her make sure you get baby back ribs, because they are the best. I left after 5 days after showing Clive I could still beat him at pool. They really didn't want me to go. I had to go back home to divorce the wife again. She was gettiog too cocky and trying to give me orders. This is the third attempt to divorce her. Something a while back, but I still remember, She said I want to live on my own, We have nothing in common. You have lost your drive and you are old and should be in an old folks home where you could be looked after. From that day on we had separate bedrooms. We are living together as strangers. We both need the money from the sale of the property at Hawthorne. I still love Teresa, But I will be moving to Las Vegas where there is no Baker Act. I am fed up getting bounced around by the Macho cops. I Don't know what Teresa is going to do. The home is priced too high, so we will never sell it. This year has been a bad year. The only good thing is, we are still alive. Teresa has so much pain in her neck and back, I don't know how she makes it to work every day. I am bipolar manic to the highest. I have met bipolar manics before. But nobody like me. It makes me laugh when the doctors say to me, Do you ever feel like hurting someone. Or hurting yourself. I am on a constant high, I have never struck a women or man, or hurt myself. I never get depressed and I have full control of my body through my brain. My last cold was in 1997 a couple of weeks after Lady Diana died. I was in England at the time. God has chosen me for something, why else would he have given me all this power at the age of 75 I thought it was to stop the wars, but how can I do that.

I am the author of this book and I hope you leam from all the mistakes that I have made in life. Nothing gets me down, I just pick myself up and on to the next project. There are a lot of con merchants out there. Its so easy to loose a million dollars like I did. I could make money easy, but I couldn't keep it. Now I am different. Citizens of Florida be aware of the Baker Act. Before you know it, you can be manhandled by the police and stuck in a mental institution and you may not even be crazy. I am moving to Las Vegas where there is no Baker Act.

CONTENTS

CHAPTER 1

There are three general Body Types

a. Mesomorph—has been known to be the perfect soldier, rarely having felt or experienced the feeling of fear. They are also great athletes, and usually very muscular.

b. Endomorph—They are known as the comedians of the bunch, funny and calm. They usually have a bit rounder shoulders and a little bit broader hips.

c. Endomorph-Endomorph can be timid at times but they are really strong hearted. They are usually slender and tall.

d. It might be possible that you can be a mix of the three general body types

e. There are even different size stomachs for instances you could be skinny and have a big stomach, or people could be chubby with small stomachs.

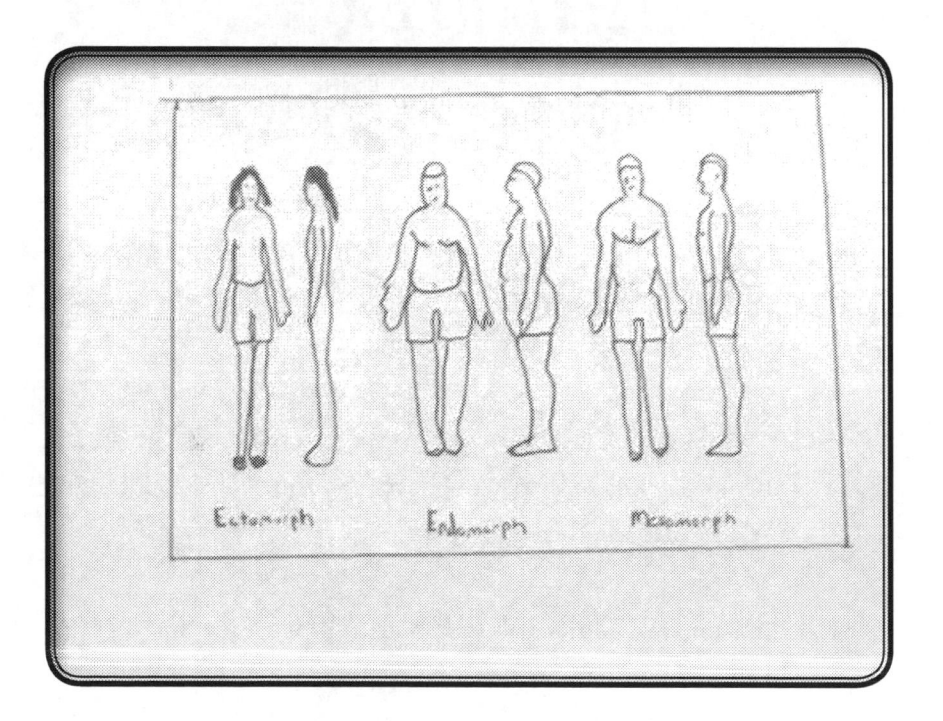

Ectomorph   Endomorph   Mesomorph

CHAPTER 2

Development in kids

From ages 1 to 5 it is more about keeping kids alive, finding food allergies and starting a health history.

From ages 5 to 10 it is a good time to introduce kids to sports, and encourage them to be active.

From ages 10 to 15 it is a good time to introduce kids to weight training. It is important to use good form.

From ages 15 to 18 it is good to develop their cardiovascular system. I recommend walking or running. This develops the heart and lungs.

At ages 18, I would recommend Martial Arts.

Side note. A good structural exercise to help kids grow is the bench-press. I also recommend squats. I also recommend weight training throughout your whole life.

BENCH PRESS

Example

CHAPTER 3

The Importance of medication and exercise

The importance of medication and exercise kind of go hand and hand if you think about it. It has been proven that a lot of people are on doctor prescribed medication. That is very common; however it is important to take the proper amount that the doctor prescribes to you. It is also important to get regular doctor check-ups so that you can stay on what works for you, and stay healthy.

It is also important to exercise on a regular basis. I have a degree from the National Personal Training Institute. I started find exercise to be about the best thing out there because it releases endorphins and it's great for your mind body and heart. It is good to set aside at least 30 minutes to an hour a day for exercise; however you should listen to your body because sometimes you may want to do more or less depending on how you are feeling

CHAPTER 4
Vitamins and Minerals

Vitamin A function promotes growth and repair of body tissues, bone formation, and healthy skin and hair. It is essential for night vision. Liver is a food source.

Vitamin E serves as an antioxidant needed for normal growth and development. Oils are a food source.

Vitamin D aids in absorption of calcium and helps to build bone mass and prevent bone loss. It helps maintain blood levels of calcium and phosphorus. Fish is food source.

Vitamin C promotes healthy cell development, wound healing, and resistance to infections. It serves as an antioxidant necessary for conversion of the inactive folic acid to the active form and makes iron available for hemoglobin synthesis. Oranges, sweet peppers are good food sources.

Vitamin K is needed for normal blood clotting and bone health. Greens are a food source. Beta carotene serves as antioxidant. Carrots are a food source.

Niacin is the coenzyme used for carbohydrate, protein and fat metabolism and proper nervous system function. High intakes can lower elevated cholesterol. Soy protein is a food source.

Pyridoxine also known as vitamin B6 is the coenzyme for protein metabolism and nervous and immune system function. It is involved in synthesis of hormones and red blood cells. Banana is a food source.

Riboflavin also known as vitamin B2 and is the coenzyme for red blood formation, nervous system functioning, and metabolism of carbohydrate, protein and fat needed for vision and may help protect against cataracts. Almonds are a food source.

Folic acid is needed for normal growth and development and red blood cell formation. It may reduce the risk of heart disease and cervical dysplasia. Oranges are food sources.

Cobalamin or vitamin B 12 is vital for blood formation and healthy nervous system. Chicken is a food source.

Biotin assists in the metabolism of fatty acids and utilization of B vitamins. Nuts are a food source.

Pantothenic acid aids in normal growth and development. Whey protein is a food sources.

MINERALS

Calcium is essential for developing and maintaining healthy bones and teeth. It assists in blood clotting, muscle contraction, and may also reduce risk of preeclampsia in pregnant woman. Juice is a food source.

Phosphorus works with calcium to develop and maintain strong bones in teeth essential for energy metabolism, DNA structure, and cell membranes.

Magnesium activates nearly 100 enzymes and helps nerves and muscles function. Constituent of bones and teeth food source is nuts.

Molybdenum is needed for metabolism of DNA and RNA and production of uric acid. Food source is milk.

Manganese is necessary for the normal development of the skeletal and connective tissues involved in metabolism of carbohydrates.

Copper is involved in iron metabolism, nervous system functioning, bone health, and synthesis of proteins. This plays a role in the pigmentation of skin, hair, and eyes.

Chromium Aids in glucose metabolism and may help regulate blood sugar in insulin levels in people with diabetes.

Iron is necessary for red blood cell formation and function. Constituent of enzyme systems. Food is source beef

Iodine is part of the thyroid hormone. It helps regulate growth, development, and energy metabolism. Food source salt.

Selenium is an essential component of a key antioxidant enzyme. It is necessary for normal growth and development and for use of iodine in thyroid function. Zinc is an essential part of more than 100 enzymes involved in digestion, metabolism, reproduction, and wound healing. Food source is lima beans.

For a diet I would recommend a doctor or a nutritionist the food pyramid is also good.

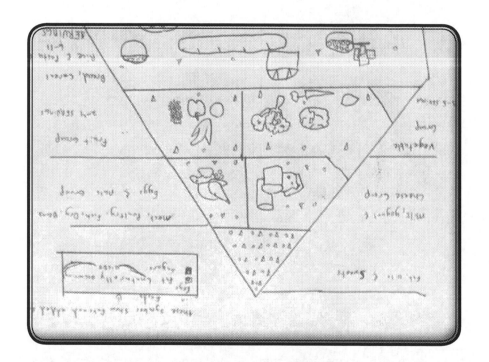

THE FOOD PYRAMID

CHAPTER 5

PART ONE EXERCISES LEGS SQUATS

FORM IS IMPORTANT. IT IS GOOD TO START WITH A
PERSONAL TRAINER OR SOMEONE WHO IS EXPERIENCED.
A SQUAT IS A GOOD BALL AND JOINT EXERCISE.

START OF A LUNGE

FINISH OF A LUNGE

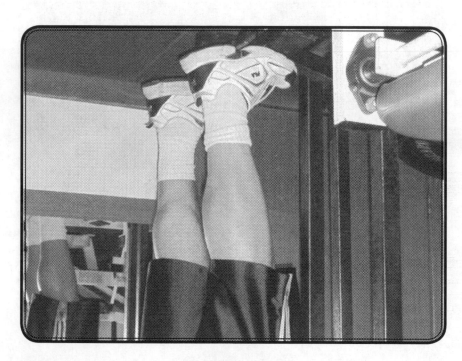

TOE RAISES

LEG CURLS

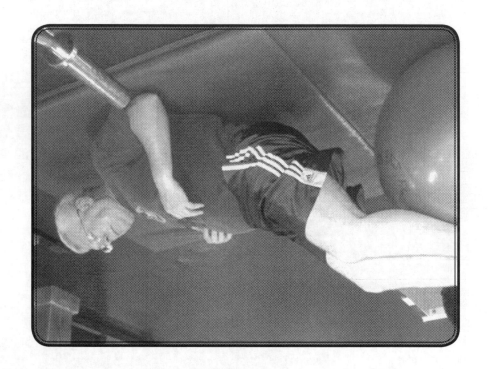

BRIDGING

CURLS

ONE ARM ONE LEG CURLS

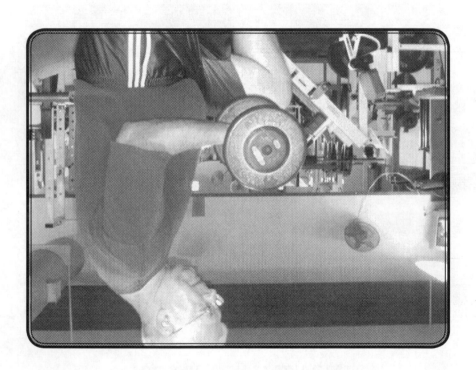

PREACHER CURLS ALMOST LIKE A LEVER YOU CAN INLINE YOURSELF

TRICEPS PUSH DOWNS

TRICEPS EXTENSIONS

SHOULDER PRESS

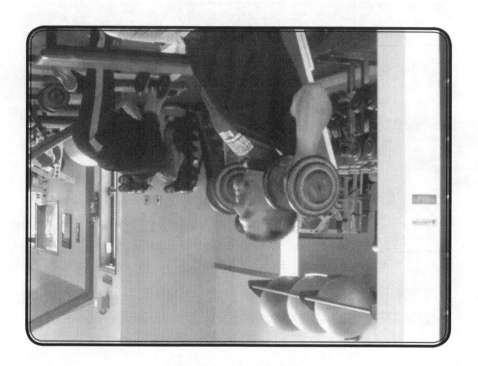

UPRIGHT ROWS

LATERAL RAISES

BENCH PRESS

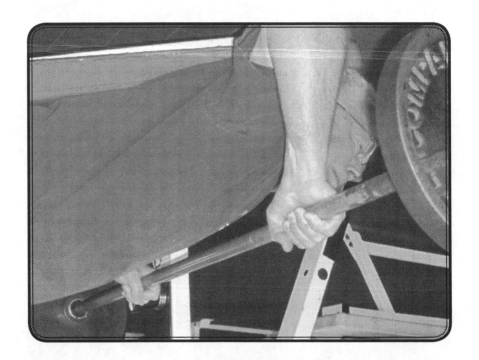

DECLINE PRESS

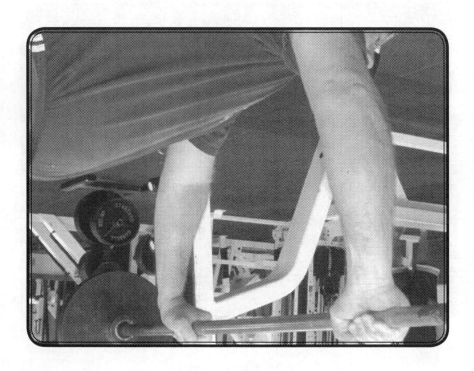

INCLINE PRESS

ONE ARM PRESS

LAT PULL DOWNS

SEATED ROWS

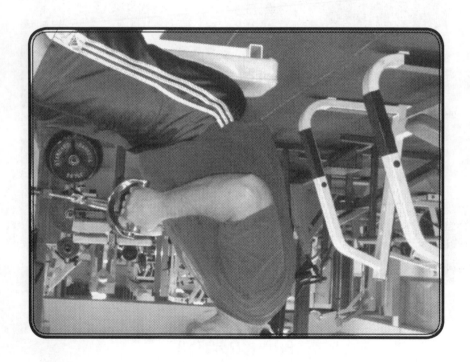

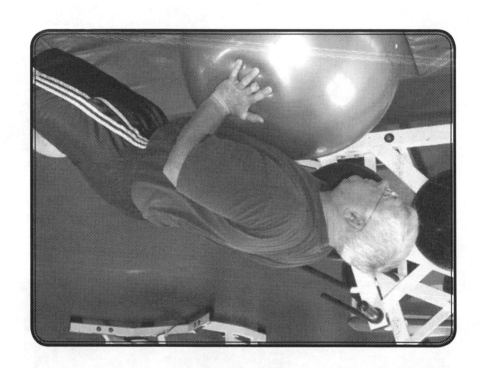

BALL PUSHUPS

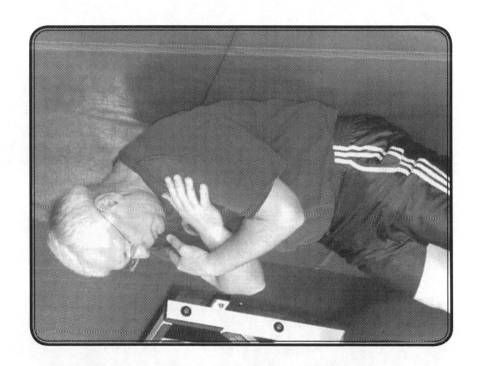

SIT UPS

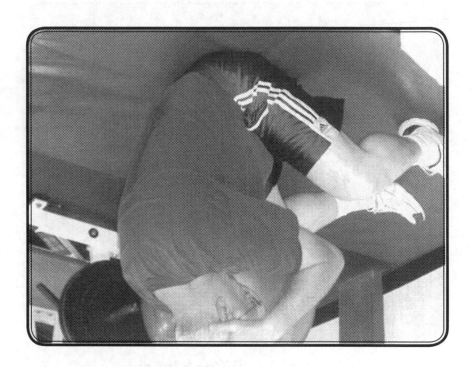

ROMAN CHAIR SIDE BENDS

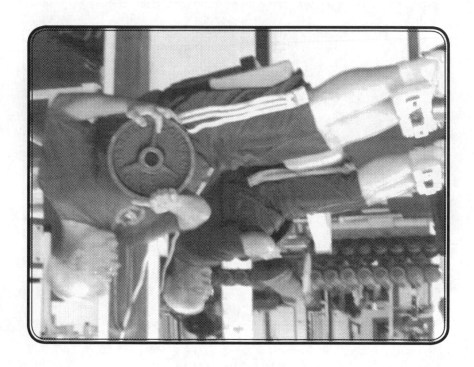

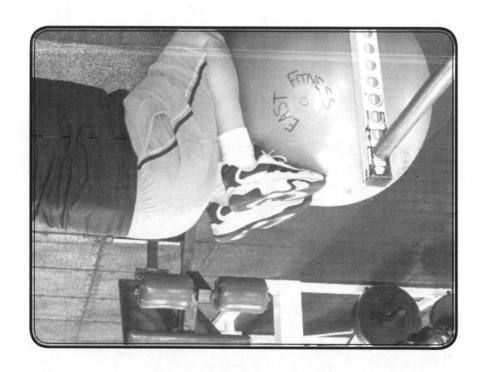

LOWER ABS WORK OUT

STRETCHING CHEST

STRETCHING WITH PRESSURE

LEG STRETCHING CAN BE FUN

STANDING LEG STRETCHS

TOUCH YOUR TOES, STRETCH,
REMEMBER TO DO YOUR CORE

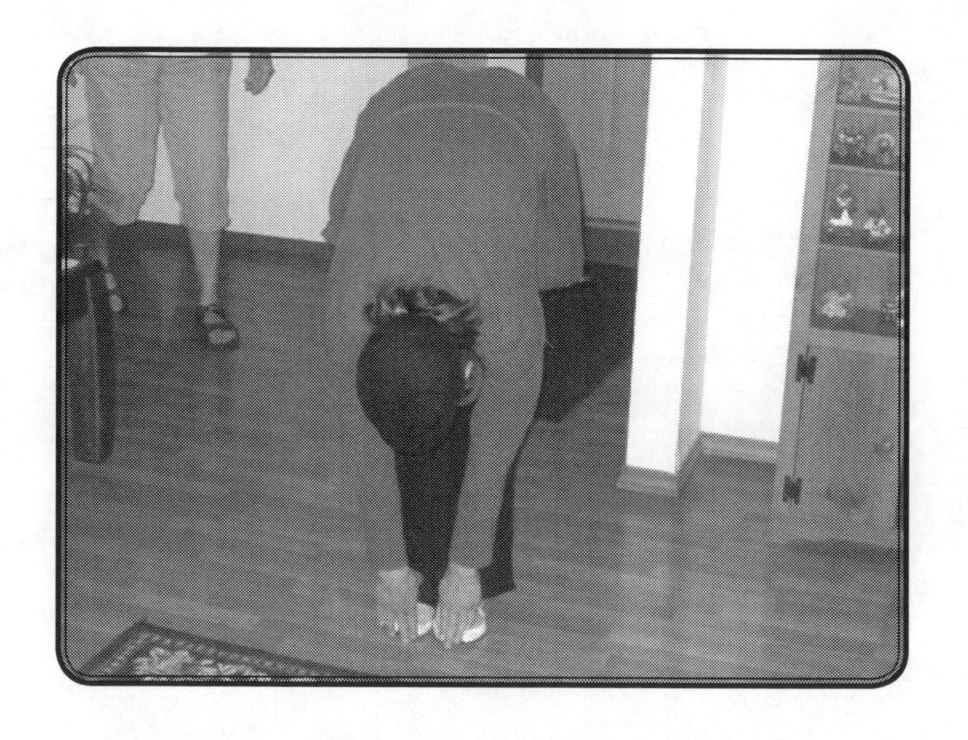

CHAPTER 6

How to become a good athlete

I found through many years of experience how to become a good athlete. Number 1 is that you need to listen to your body. Number 2 is weight training because it is really good for your body and your overall health. Number 3 is playing a variety of sports. Number 4 is that a combination of these 3 things will make you a good athlete.

Sample Routine:
Warm up with 10 to 25 minutes of basketball.
Next I recommend a full body workout using weight training.
For a cool down I would recommend short quick movements such as sparing with a bag for a minute or two.
Then I recommend taking a slow walk to cool down.

On a side note, if you choose to do cardio it should be short, quick movements, or whatever you feel you need to stay healthy. The reason for this is that we have fast and slow twitch muscles. To be a good athlete you want to use your fast twitch muscles. In this book we are going more for sports such as football, basketball, racquetball, and

baseball. Obviously if you want to do cross-country, or run a marathon those are also great athletes. I would recommend that you start with a personal trainer that specializes in cardio and running, and remember it is important to stretch.

CHAPTER 7

Beginning weight training

Sample Routine: 5 to 10 mins. on a bike to warm up plus 5 to 10 mins. Of stretching upper body: bench press incline, press lat pull downs with sit ups, one arm rows with back extensions, shoulder press next upright rows or lateral raises, then curls with triceps extensions, forearm curls or reverse curls.

5 to 10 mins on a bike or treadmill to cool down along with 5 to 10 mins stretching. You can always do more are less cardio if you fell you need it.

Legs: 5 to 10 mins. Of jump rope along with 5 to 10 mins. Stretching Squats, leg curls, leg extension, leg presses, toe raises, leg adductions and abductions, dead lifts, seated calf raises.

5 to 10 mins on a bike to cool down along with 5 to 10 mins stretching

There are four different routines; Strength is 1 to 6 reps with a 2 to 5 mins rest. Power is 1to 2 reps with a 2 to 5 mins rest. Hypertrophy 6 to 12 reps with a 30 to 90 seconds rest and Muscular endurance is 12 to 25 reps with 30 seconds rest or less.

CHAPTER 8

How to become a good athlete part 2

I found martial arts good for self disciple and over all control, also I found 1 of things martial arts teaches is it's better not to fight, but it gives kids and adults confidence to win and call the cops, if attacked. Also it gives people strength and flexibility. I also was told by a martial art teacher, it's a left and right brain exercise. All good to know if you what to be physically and mentally prepared to be an athlete. Also I found using your own body weight is a good way to be a good athlete also good for you're over all heath. Things like yoga, Pilates, ball work are good to add in a couple times a week. Examples are at the bottom.

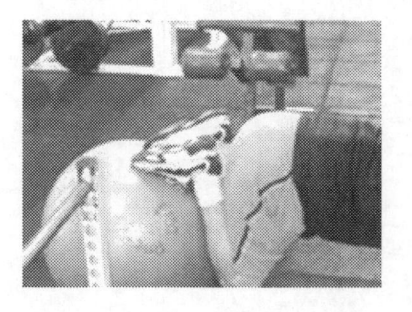
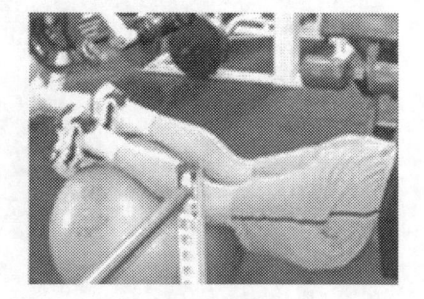

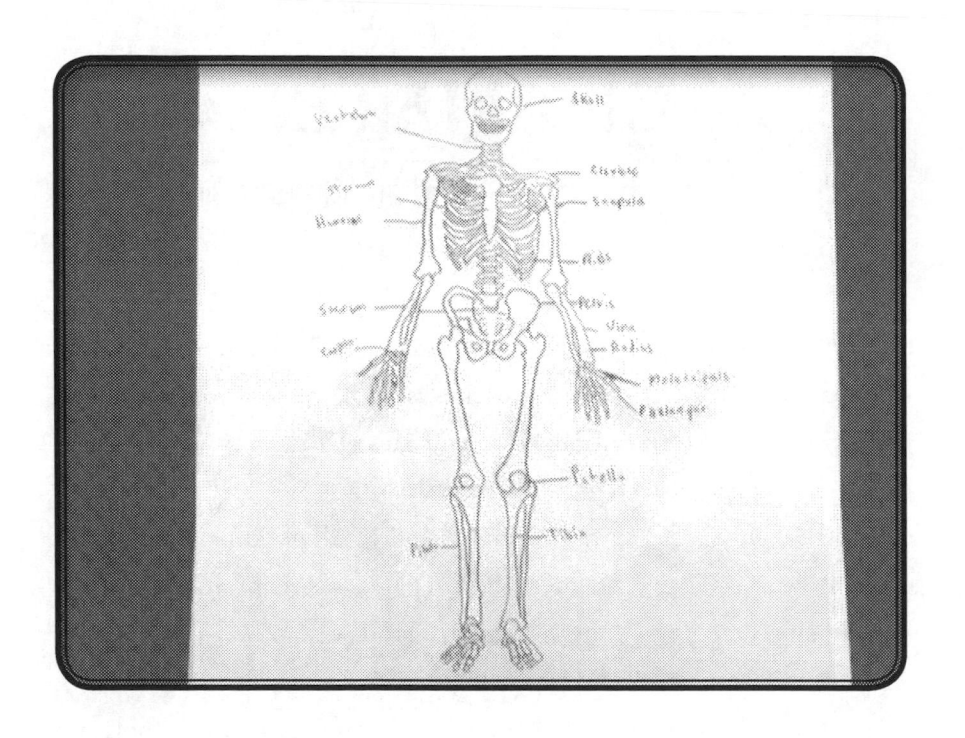

Chapter 9 I would recommend everybody reads a bones & anatomy
book to further health knowledge.

CHAPTER 9

WAYS TWO FIGHT STESS

1. EXERCISE
2. GO TO CHURCH
3. GO FOR WALK
4. GO FOR WALK AT A DUCK POND OR PARK
5. WATCH A MOVIE
6. GET A ANIMAL LIKE A DOG OR CAT
7. READ A BOOK
8. HAVE FAITH THAT EVERTHING WILL WORK OUT THE WAY YOU WANT IT TO

CHAPTER 10

RECOMENDATIONS

1. IF YOU WANT TO BE RUNNER FIND A PERSONAL TRAINER THAT SPECIALIZED IN CARDIO AND RUNING
2. MAKE HEALTHY SELECTIONS
3. START WITH A PERSONAL TRAINER.
4. GET LOTS OF REST.
5. HEALTH TRADE SCHOOLS ARE A GOOD PLACE TO START
6. DO LOTS OF STRETCHING.

ABOUT THE AUTHOR

Eric received a degree at national personal training institute and likes a variety of sports.

ISBN: 978-1-4269-9645-0 (sc)
ISBN: 978-1-4269-9646-7 (e)

Trafford rev. 09/27/2011

Trafford. www.trafford.com
PUBLISHING

North America & international
toll-free: 1 888 232 4444 (USA & Canada)
phone: 250 383 6864 ♦ fax: 812 355 4082

FITNESS
THE
SIMPLE WAY
TO A
BETTER
LIFE

August 10

2011

Start getting healthy today

THREE GENERAL BODY TYPES
GOOD RECOMMENDATIONS

FITNESS AND HEALTH

By ERIC R PELLATZ

Foreword

This book continues the saga of the Tracey-O'Neill—the life and times of an Irish-French Canadian (with a smattering of American Indian, Spanish, and Swiss ancestors). When I completed the two earlier volumes of this trilogy, *Stands of Memory* and *Strands of Memory Revisited,* I thought that I had exhausted the subject, that there was nothing left to write about. I was very wrong. I have remembered so many subjects, memories, incidents, and mental meanderings in the few years since their publication that I now have the contents of several additional books—but time and my advancing age will prevent the extension of this writing genre from continuing indefinitely. So this volume must be my swan song, rather than just an encore or curtain call. Regretfully, I have neither enough time nor the energy to undertake another volume.

During my long life, I have stored information and memories from my experiences. Since I started writing, I have tried to make some sense of those events. It's my belief that, when we are not able to understand fully the events that have occurred, we externalize the information. By doing so, we gain an entirely different perspective, thus allowing us to think more clearly and rationally about the difficult or perplexing events and emotions in our lives. Verse is my way of externalizing and comprehending more fully my thoughts and feelings about my experiences. But it is also an invaluable means of releasing pent-up emotions and for painting beautiful, sad, or joyous pictures with words.

But the process and the advantages of externalizing experiences are not the only reason I write verse. I also use poetry as a powerful tool for sharing sometimes confusing and other times perfectly clear concepts. My intentions also vary. I often simply want to share something that has touched me in some profound way, or I my use the venue to get help in allaying uncertainty, anxiety, or ambiguity. That is, poetry can be therapeutic for both the author and readers, allowing them to work through the issues and problems in their lives to find clarity, consolation, and peace, even solutions.

Fortunately for me, poetry as an art form now allows writers to record their life experiences and share their poetic vision with others in a great variety of styles and forms, from more or less intricate rhyme schemes to free verse, a complete lack of rhyme. Although none of the poems in this collection involve complex rhyming, they include both verse in simple rhyming and straight-forward narrative forms.

In some of my verses, I am trying to speak to certain readers more than others—to children, young parents, and older people who share many of my problems and experiences. Verse also affords an opportunity to reevaluate ourselves, our relationships with others, and our status and position in life. However, it always important for readers to keep in mind that each verse is the voice of a poet trying to reach them in some palpable way. Yet, I believe that in some way almost every reader can relate to the topics and themes expressed in my poems. They address important and often timely issues and topics that might otherwise be ignored. So, I hope that each verse conveys its own message and provides a means of expression for diverse attitudes and fresh insights.

Once again, these poems. whether rhyming or free verse, are the songs of my life, cataloged under the headings of love. family, friendship, war, nature, and life and death. Writing them was an emotional challenge—essentially reliving difficult times, happy events—joyful, cheerful, thorny, testing, frustrating, painful, formidable experiences—important and often timely issues and topics that might otherwise be ignored. So, I hope that each verse conveys its own message and provides a means of expression for diverse attitudes and fresh insights.

In summary, the verses that follow represent the distilled essence of my long life—impressions and visions that I hope will inspire readers at this point in their journey through life. I hope that they enjoy them.

WRT

Listen to these words
They are the songs of my life
Store them in your heart

Love

Love and family,
Friendship, War, Nature, and
Life,
These are my themes

Love

Here are my thoughts about us on your birthday.
I believe that we share these blessings:
Being in love—a magical place.
Needing love—a common place.
Giving love—a marvelous place.
Accepting love—a necessary place.
Being loved—a special place.
Sharing love—an exceptional place.
We both live in those wondrous places,
settings that make life not only worth living
but also infinitely fulfilling.
I am totally grateful to you for those gifts
and the years that I have enjoyed them.
I'm hoping for another decade or more
to revel in sharing them with my love.

For My Love on Her 69th Birthday

It's hard to believe that another year has passed.
In many ways it has not been an auspicious one,
It has been marked by accidents and illnesses
for both of us:
For you, a broken hip, surgery, overwhelming pain.
a damaged shoulder,
and problems with people at Cumberland Farms.
For me, it has meant four months of misery
caused by an undiagnosed and unidentified illness,
accompanied by multiple tests and medical procedures
that revealed nothing
and did nothing to relieve the shortness of breath,
light headedness, and piercing back pain.
Despite those problems,
there were many bright spots and reasons for thanks.
First, our love or each other grew and blossomed,
and our happiness was ever-present
when we shared time together.
So, the balance between negatives and positives
in our relationship and experiences
remained on the plus side.
For that, I am deeply grateful to you
because it reflects your concern for and about me,
which mirrors my concern for and about you,
with love, gratitude, and this special prayer:
May you see God's Light
on the path ahead
when the road you walk is dark.
May you always remember
when shadows fall
you do not walk alone.

For My Love on Valentine's Day

This has been a very harrowing year for you:
the alarming diagnosis,
followed by painful surgery,
weeks of radiation therapy, chemotherapy,
and yet another surgical procedure.
You have endured this arduous time
with courage, fortitude, and grace,
You are a remarkable woman,
a role model that few women could emulate.
You have been the love of my senior years.
I realize that I am often quick tempered,
short on patience, and exasperatingly difficult.
But, believe me my heart is in the right place
—completely and entirely with you—
and has never left there for the past nine years.
You have been a prodigious blessing in my life,
the primary source of my well-being and happiness!
So, please forgive what you rightly
view as badgering you about your habit.
My behavior is simply an indication, even evidence,
of my love for you, and my deep concern
for your health, welfare, and longevity.
I need you to be around for many years to come.
Your surgeon's report about the absence of evidence
of the spread of the dreaded malignant cells
takes care of one element that determines your life span.
The other is the only source of contention between us.
So, please always remember this as I invariably do:
If love means happiness, then how can I start
to count all the smiles
you've brought to my heart?

For EMB

Here are my wishes
for you on Valentine's Day:

Sunlight and a rainbow after showers;
lots and lots of smiles
and many wonderful, happy hours.
Flowers at your door,
good fortune and laughter, too.
Friendships that never end,
every day your whole life through.

Wishing you a day of extraordinary miracles;
a day full of things to delight in;
a day in which everything is perfect;
a day of knowing that you're someone special;
a day of tranquility, happiness, and joy.

Wishing that you hold tightly
to your memories for comfort;
that you lean on your friends,
and especially on me for strength,
and remember always
how much you are loved.

These words are filled with thoughts,
understanding, and more than anything else,
with hope that every day ahead
will bring a large measure of love
and days filled with wishes come true.

My Continuing Christmas Gift

How delighted I was to meet you
at Way"s in 2001.
How fortuitous it was to meet
when I needed someone so badly.
How charmed I was to see you looking
so young and attractive
How gratified I was when you accepted
my dinner invitation.
How intrigued I was by your accent.
How surprised I was by your extensive
English vocabulary
How comfortable I was
exchanging information
about our families.
How contented I feel
when we are together.
How captivated I was
when we kissed.
How fascinated I was
by your energy and interests.
How pleased I was
to meet your son and granddaughter.
How elated I was when you told me
you loved me,
How ecstatic and revived I was
after every meeting with you.
How rhapsodic, euphoric, and joyful
I felt long after.
How lucky and happy
I am to have you.
How blessed I am
to have spent my last years with you

For Else-Marie on Valentine's Day

Today is another very special day for you, Clarence,
and Kiana—and, most of all, for me,
It is a day to recall the wonderful days, weeks,
months, yes, even years,
that we have both enjoyed and benefited from each other.

To me, those years were bona fide blessings—
a new life, an inspiration, renewed vitality, additional years—
outcomes of a wonderful relationship that I never expected,
had not earned, and undoubtedly did not deserve.

So, here we are, half way through our tenth year
an era that began August 3, 2001
and has matured and improved over time.
So, for my Else-Marie, may there always be
bright stars and a full moon above you,
dazzling sunshine to warm you,
scores of faithful friends to love you,
genuine laughter to prevail over every care,
and in your heart a song, a cheerful melody
to entertain you and give you
heartfelt joy and happiness everywhere you go
through the length of days for rest of your life.

Always remember this:
Even when the words are not spoken or written,
my thoughts are always full of best wishes for you.
My love for you is always in my heart
to tell you how much you're loved all year through.

For Else-Marie at Christmas

Do you know how much you are loved?
Not only by me, but also by my whole family
sons, daughters, spouses, in-laws,
grandchildren, great grandchildren
—and close friends,—a total of more than 28 people!
Count them yourself.

We all want the very best for you,
this year and for many many years to come.
So, please remember that every day
and keep the promise you made to me Monday.

Remember this:
When you're with me, I'm happy.
When you're not here with me,
I miss you terribly.
When I can't reach you by phone,
I'm heartbroken,
When you are ill for whatever reason,
I'm miserable and depressed.

So, stay well!
Be with me as much as possible,
continually stay in touch,
unfailingly keep your promises
and faithfully love me
as I love and respect you.
my perpetual and incomparable paramour.

A Thank You to Kathleen

Believe me the 56 years we had together
were both wonderful and wondrous.
Following difficult childhood and teen years,
when I met you, I finally became an alive and happy man,
although far from a perfect one.

I know that I was not always good company—
sometimes ill-tempered and petulant
and all too often insensitive and inconsiderate.
Nonetheless, you were always patient and understanding
—a blessing in my life—the core of my being
and the primary source of my happiness, joy,
and contentment for almost six decades.

You were always there for me—caring, concerned,
involved, supportive, and loving.
Without you, I would have been a nobody
and achieved nothing of any consequence.

So, from the bottom of my heart
I thank you for those wonderful years
and for the things you helped me to accomplish—
including our six children, twelve grand children,
and two (soon to be three) great grandchildren
I love you and miss you every day of my life,
my Kay, the perfect wife and mother.

For EMB on Her 70th Birthday

This is another important milestone for you.
It is also a very significant anniversary for me—
not because November 19th itself
is more important than August 3, 2001
(when we met at Ways),
August 20 (our dinner date at Polcari's),
or September 2,
when I made dinner for you at my house.
It's of great consequence because it celebrates
the tenth anniversary we have been together
on your birthday.
Believe me, those ten anniversaries have been
both wonderful and wondrous,
simply because I became alive and happy
after a very desolate and depressing four years
following the death of my wife—
and what I believe was a very difficult year for you,
following the passing of your husband, Clarence.
I know that I have not always been good company,
due mainly to my age, illnesses, and physical problems,
(resulting in grumpiness, crabbiness, and petulance)
but also due to my deep
and abiding concern for your well-being.
So, let me make it clear that you have been
a blessing in my life
and the primary source of my happiness, joy,
and contentment for almost a decade.
You have always been there for me—
caring, concerned, involved, and loving.
From the bottom of my heart,
I thank you for those gifts and wish you a
Happy Birthday

Other Ways to "Say" I Love You

Husband to Wife

Sending or bringing flowers
Writing a love letter or poem
Giving her an unexpected kiss and hug
Serving her breakfast in bed
Bathing the kids and putting them to bed
Changing the baby's diaper
Staying fit, healthy, and clean
Going shopping with her
Minding the kids while she sleeps in
Cooking Saturday or Sunday breakfast
Clearing the table and doing the dishes
Complimenting her appearance/hairdo/cooking

Wife to Husband

Making his favorite meals
Inviting his "buddy" to dinner
Showing interest in his job/hobbies
Writing a poem or love letter
Being an exemplary mother
Helping with spring and fall yard cleanups
Accompanying him to sports events
Keeping a clean and well organized home
Staying fit, healthy, and seductive
Dressing or undressing provocatively
Engaging in impulsive expressions of affection
Sharing responsibility for financial well being

Family

A good dad is worth
More than one hundred
teachers
In a youngster's life

For Maura on the Big 55

I can't believe it
because you don't look or act the part
of a middle-aged woman.
Without inside knowledge,
I'd give you 30 at most.
But then I'd have to revise the number upward
because of your mature mind
—and again downward because of your
physical attributes and youthful outlook.

In any case, know that I admire you
as well as love you to distraction.
Similarly, your daughter, all of your siblings,
nieces, nephews, friends, coworkers, and students
love you and love to be with you.
Your demeanor, caring nature, and generosity
in one person are truly gifts to be treasured.

Since your Mom died, you have been my anchor,
my best friend and stalwart companion.
How I have looked forward to your visits
and especially your summers with me
during the last four years!

My hope is that I will be given several more years
to enjoy your daily company at the Cape,
the place that I love
the most of all the places I have lived in my long life.

For Great Grandson David Matthew

You will not understand these words for several years.
But, if you keep this bit of verse until you are older,
They will mean something
that I hope will be important to you.
Yesterday, November 2, 2010, was a special day
for your Mom and Dad, your sister Grace,
your aunt Mikie, your Tracey and Munson grandparents
and other relatives, and for you, and for me, too.
So, here are a few thoughts.
whether they are true gems or not
will someday be totally up to you.
* * *

Never doubt for a moment how much it means to me,
to have you as a great grandson.
There's a special sort of feeling
that's warm and loving, too.
a special kind of pride,
that comes with every thought of you.
Whatever makes you sad, whatever makes you glad,
to your Great Grand Poppi matter greatly.
I hope and pray that many happy days are to come
for you, those named above,
and whomever else you choose.
And always remember this:
Even when words are not spoken or written,
my love for you is always in my heart.
So, these special thoughts on your birth
are full of hugs for you
to let you know how much
you're loved all year through.
* * *

I close with this Irish Blessing:
May you live a long life full of gladness and health
with a pocket full of gold as the least of your wealth,
May dreams you hold dear be those which come true,
And the love that you spread keeps returning to you.
*   *   *
Note: I write this verse the day after your were born—November 2, 2010. I have the honor and privilege of being your great grandfather. At age 88. I am probably your oldest living blood relative. I hope that we shall meet at least once before I leave for "the other side," but there are no guarantees about such a meeting. None-the-less, I want you to know that I have high hopes, best wishes, and heart-felt prayers that you have a healthy, productive, and wonderful life. Although we are separated by the full width of a continent, care, concern, and love easily and readily span such a distance. Wishing can make it so!
Love,
Great Grand Poppi
William Raymond Tracey

For Sean T. on His 51st Birthday

My heart is filled with affection this special day—
my emotions are so strong that I cannot say
all of the things that should be in this rondelet
to make it a special and memorable bouquet
for my youngest son to remember every day.
Our lives are so busy that many times we find
we haven't even addressed the things
we've often had in mind.
That's why this day is welcome
for the perfect chance it brings
to wish for someone as suave as you
the best of life's good things.!

You are a very unique man:
Gifted and creative
Skillful and talented
Professional and self-disciplined
Imaginative and perspicacious
Caring and helpful
Faithful and persuasive
Respected and loved

In short, you are a role model for
husbands and fathers.
May your days be touched
by more than a bit of Irish luck.
brightened by a song in your heart,
and warmed by the smiles
of the people you love.

How blessed I am, how grateful I am
that you are my son and also my friend!

For Katie on Her 16ᵗʰ Birthday

Today is another special day
for your Mom and Dad, L.B., and Tim,
for you. and for me, too.
So, here are a few thoughts.
Whether they are true gems or not
is really up to you.
*   *   *
Never doubt for a moment
how much it has meant to me,
and will always mean to me,
to have you as a granddaughter.
There's a special sort of feeling
that's warm and loving, too.
a special kind of pride,
that comes with every thought of you.
Whatever makes you sad,
whatever makes you glad,
to your Poppi matter greatly.
I hope and pray nightly
that many happy days are to come
for you, those named above,
and whomever else you choose.
*   *   *
And always remember this:
Even when words are not spoken or written,
my love for you is always in my heart.
So, these special thoughts on your birthday
are full of hugs for you.
And always remember: Whatever happens,
regardless of the season, happens for a reason.

For Leah on Her Birthday

This is another auspicious day for you and Sean—
and now for me too!
For it is now my privilege to call you
my daughter-in-law.
And I do that with great pride
and thanks for that happy and loving relationship
between you and my special grandson,
the one who was favored above all others
by my wife, his Nanni, Kathleen.
Here are my prayers for my lovely and loving
daughter-in-law:
May there always be:
Bright stars and a full moon above you.
Dazzling sunshine to warm you.
Scores of faithful friends to love you,
.Genuine laughter to prevail over your every care.
And in your heart a song, a cheerful melody.
With heartfelt joy and happiness everywhere,
All your whole life long.
Happy Birthday!

For Tamra on Her 36th Birthday

Where have the years gone?
It seems like only yesterday
that Kaila was born.
And only a few short months before
that you and James were married.
And only a few years earlier,
that you were a blue-eyed, fair-skinned,
bright and lovely little girl—
although also an accomplished drama princess
(rather than a queen).

And where did your college years
at UMass Lowell go,
when your Nanni was still here?
And also your graduation
with an MBA from UNH,
which I attended without her
because she was gone.
So, we should be thankful
for so many good years!
But, there are many more to come for you
and your beautiful and talented daughter.

So, here are my wishes and prayers for you:
May your dreams blossom as vibrantly as flowers.
May your heart be as light
as a happy song.
May every day bring you bright happy hours
that stay with you all year long.

For Tim on His 20th Birthday

Today is another special day
for you and for me.
So, here are a few thoughts.
Whether they are true gems or not
is really up to thee.
Every man has to face his demons,
exploit his strengths,
come to grips with his failings,
and accept love in his life.
Success should never be measured
in dollars earned.
A better metric is the amount
of satisfaction you feel
when you achieve a goal.
According to actuaries,
at age 20 you have lived
one fourth of the years you will have.
Life is very much a crapshoot,
so live for today
as if it were your last day on earth.
Happiness is very elusive,
but you'll know it when you find it.
The heaviest thing anyone can carry
is a grudge against another.
May the dreams you hold dearest
be those that come true,
and the love that you spread,
keep returning to you.
And always remember:
Whatever happens,
happens for a reason.
HAPPY BIRTHDAY!

For Kathy on Her Birthday

Today is the day we celebrate you—
the wonderful person you are, so loving and true—
the difference you make for so many others
that you don't even know
and the good things that happen wherever you go.
You are a very special person.
I hope that your day will be filled with reminders
of what a exceptional person you are—
to me and to all who know and love you—
Dennis, Tamra, Sean, Kaila, your siblings,
nieces and nephews, in-laws, friends, colleagues.
and the kids and student teachers
you so skillfully and lovingly taught and mentored
over so many years.
Let me underscore the faith and affection you inspire,
the hearts and minds that you uplift,
that, although it is <u>your</u> birthday,
those around and near you,
are the ones who <u>receive</u> the gift.
HAPPY BIRTHDAY!

On Bill's Birthday

I'm so proud of you!
You did it!
You have proved again
that I am "invariably right"
in critically important matters—
at least I have always tried
to convey that impression
to my progeny
(or deluded myself into believing it),
.Regardless, you have achieved a goal
that has proved to be unreachable
by most people without intensive therapy
and daily contact and support
with and from a group such as AA:
That unique state is called Sobriety.
You know, even better than I,
how difficult a journey that can be.
You have endured and survived
the problems associated with alcoholism,
including hospitalization—and near death
with the delirium tremens (DTs).
There is little doubt in my mind
that at least in part the origin
of your affliction was genetic:
Your grandfather died due to alcoholism,
and eight years ago I was a borderline alcoholic
with severe pancreatitis,
a result of ample amounts of alcohol consumed daily
during my 1600 "Happy Hour."
Upon advice of my gastroenterologist.

I went on the wagon immediately and permanently
—no liquor, no wine, no beer, no ale
no time, nowhere—for life.
Although the euphemism, "recovering alcoholic"
is widely used to describe our current status,
its true meaning is that we consider ourselves
to be "continuing our therapy,"
which is complete abstinence
from drinkable alcohol in all of its forms forever.
That is both our prescription and our destiny.
Let me not leave this subject
without giving credit and my thanks to Kim,
who stood by you daily throughout your ordeal.
She is a remarkable and beautiful woman.
You are indeed fortunate to have her in your life.
Let me say again that I am very proud of my oldest son
and happy that he had the fortitude and determination
to overcome a very fierce and formidable adversary.
I am happy to declare this truth
to everyone who reads this verse:
How blessed I am,
how fortunate I've been,
that your are not only my oldest son
but also my friend!
*   *   *

And I end with this Irish blessing:
May your troubles be less,
and your blessings be more.
And nothing but happiness,
come through your door.
HAPPY BIRTHDAY!

For Joanne

How blessed I am,
how fortunate I've been
that you are my daughter-in-law
and also my friend!
To some, if not many,
I suspect that you are an enigma:
Outgoing, personable, attractive,
warm, friendly, and caring.
but also flippant, naughty,
obstreperous, earthy, irreverent,
and charmingly insulting.
Nonetheless, this is for someone very special,
a wish for you today and all year through:
May God in His goodness
send blessings your way,
sunshine to cheer you and brighten your day,
faith to inspire you, hope to impart
a feeling of gladness and peace in your heart.
This is the kind of wish that comes from the heart.
It's certainly off to a wonderful start.
So you can be sure this wish just for you
holds so much love it's bound to come true.
Know this, even without
your repeated prompting and warnings
of dire consequences
if I omit this admission:
I love you as my third daughter.
and have from the beginning of our association.
So, may your cup be never empty
May your heart be ever full.
That is my prayer for you
And that is no bull.

For Kaila on Her 4th Birthday

You have a special place in my heart—
one that belongs only to you,
my beautiful, bright, loving,
and first great granddaughter,
It is a special place saved
for the times we have known at Cape Cod.,
a special place for events we have shared,
and a place for wishes and dreams, too.
But the warmest place within my heart
is a wish for good health and happiness for you.
So, not a single day goes by wherever I am
that I don't thank God
and remember how lucky I am
to have a loving great granddaughter like you.
HAPPY BIRTHDAY!

Haiku for Kaila

Take care of yourself
Enjoy healthful food and drink
Live a lengthy life

For LB on His 23rd Birthday

At the risk of turning you off with the thoughts
I expressed earlier in letterform,
I shall repeat my viewpoints about life and work.
*   *   *
Any job, no matter how boring or low paying,
Is a much better option
Than sitting around,
wishing that things were better,
and doing absolutely nothing.

As a matter of fact,
Mundane jobs are valuable learning experiences.
They develop stamina and fortitude,
as well as the resolve to do something
more challenging and remunerative
as one's chosen life work.
The road to doing just that is education—
as a minimum an associate's degree
and preferably a bachelor's or master's.
And it matters little in which field
the degree is granted,
except for specific professions.
The key is the degree itself for the discipline
and study habits it engenders.

Don't depend n anyone for the money
to pay for your education.
If you earn it yourself,
it will be more satisfying.
So, William Raymond Tracey, III, go for it!
Time will pass more quickly as you age.

Your 30th birthday will be here
before you know it!
So get with the program now!
*   *   *

Here are my wishes for you on your special day:
good fortune at your door, and laughter, too;
new friendships to warm your heart
and old friendships that never end,
every day your whole life through.
Wishing you a day of extraordinary miracles;
a day full of things to delight in;
a day in which everything is perfect;
a day of knowing that you're someone special
to your Mom and Dad, Tim and Katie,
and to your Poppi
HAPPY BIRTHDAY!

Haiku for L.B.

The key to good health:
Stay positive in outlook
Don't sweat the small stuff

An analog man
In today's digital world
A bad place to be

For Laine on Her 26th Birthday

Another year has elapsed,
and again, as in years past,
it entailed some momentous decisions.
Although none were life threatening.
some were probably intimidating,
and at least two were life changing.

One of those judgments will have
a direct effect on you career—
your pursuit of a master of education degree
and the vital profession of teaching.
The other decision relates to your
choice of a mate—a husband
and potential father of your children.

I commend you for, wholeheartedly endorse,
and joyfully applaud both of those decisions.
Fortunately, I do this after the fact
and had nothing to do with your choices
—except observe as an exceptionally interested
and genuinely concerned grandfather.

Bright, beautiful, and multi-talented,
you have much to give as a teacher
and later, as a wife and mother.
I hope to see you achieve both goals,
so I plan to stay around until you do.
However, the odds are against me—
today is my 88th birthday,
the longest life span of any of my forebears
on either side of my family.
My mother was one of 14
my father was one of 7,
and I am the lone survivor of 8 siblings.

Always remember this:
Even when the words are not spoken
or written,
these special thoughts on your birthday
are full of hugs for you.
My love for you is always in my heart.
to let you know how much you're loved
all year through.

For Maura Gail

Today, your birthday, is the day
when we celebrate YOU—
the woman that you are, so authentic,
caring, and true.
The differences you make
that you don't even know
and the good things that happen wherever you go.
the trust you inspire, the hearts you uplift,
although it's your birthday,
it's your family and friends that get those gifts.
It takes thoughtfulness and caring
to be the kind of woman you are.
Perhaps you don't realize day after day
the joy you bring to us in your warm-hearted way.
That's why you are wished happiness
today and every day.
No amount of money or other treasure
could ever be as special as my Maura is to me.
So lucky am I to have a daughter like you:
Your smiles and laughter
your cooking and housekeeping,
your companionship and love, too.
My heart could not
be happier or luckier than that.
So, even when the words go unspoken,
my love for you is always in my heart.

Haiku for Maura

Remember this truth
Happiness lies in the heart
Not in the venue

For Jackie on Her 33rd Birthday

Today marks another auspicious year for you--
a happy, talented, lovely, and loving
young wife and mother.
You were a joy to be with on those
(all too few occasions)
when I was able to be with you.
I regret that I was not privileged to observe
as you progressed from childhood to adulthood
due to the great distance that separated us.
Unfortunately, that situation cannot be remedied
for Grace, my second great granddaughter, and me.
However, it does not diminish the love in my heart
for my beautiful and brilliant great grandchild
just as it did not lessen the affection and attachment
I felt and continue to have
for her mother, my second granddaughter.
Here is an old Irish prayer
to protect you on your life journey.
May your days be touched
by more than a bit of Irish luck.
brightened by a song in your heart,
and warmed by the smiles
of the people you love.
Happy Birthday!

Haiku for Jackie

You are in my prayers
In a warm and special way
Today and all days

For Kaylyn on Her 10th Birthday

I find it hard to believe that you have reached
the first set of double figures that tell your age.
But the years pass quickly when you are old—
and still enjoying life, your family,
and having fun daily.
Do you know that you have someone in Heaven
who loves you completely and unconditionally?
Her name is Kathleen, my wife and your Nanni.
She was such a beautiful, funny, and loving lady!
Although you were born after she had gone to Heaven,
She knows you, your sister, Kolby,
your cousins, Victor, Siara, Kaila, and Grace,
four of her 12 grandchildren and three great grandchildren
who were born after she left us.
How she would have enjoyed rocking
and singing to you
when you were a baby—and playing with you now!
Those were wonderful times
that both she and you missed.
But she has been watching over you
and protecting you since you were born—
and she will continue to do that
for the rest of your life.
Your Nanni also left some permanent records
for you—

Remembering . . . . the story of her life on CDs
and in book form,
even a VCR of our wedding—
as well as my memories of her
in the many poems I have written
for her over the years—
and included in my books of poetry,
Strands of Memory and *Strands of Memory Revisited.*
So, remember your Nanni,
and ask her for her help when you need it—
as your Dad, uncles, aunts, cousins,
many of her friends, and your Poppi do so often.

Haiku for Kaylyn

Kaylyn is so cool
Because she is genuine
And very lovely

Loving is a gift
Receiving love a blessing
Be grateful for both

A Note to My Nephew Frank

As I said in my recent letter, you did a masterful job
with arrangements for your Mother's funeral.
Everything was in good taste,
and your plans made it easy
for relatives and friends to celebrate her life.
It may seem to be an inappropriate time
to celebrate your birthday—but it's not.
It's always right and proper to be thankful
for another year of life,
a gift from God, at any time,
for any one, and at every age.
Essentially, you have lived your adult life
for your Mother.
That is an uncommon gift for anyone
to bestow on another.
But, the time is ripe for you to do
whatever it is that you want and can do
with the remaining years of your life.
In other words, you should do
whatever fulfills you
and makes you content, even happy.
You have the gifts of an excellent intellect,
academic credentials,
and intelligence-related (or required)
educational background and, in most cases,
the experience needed for success
in many fields of endeavor.
Your two degrees in education
and experience in the Boston public schools,
as well as your knowledge and experience
in the Catholic faith

(probably at or near the level of the deaconate)
make you a creditable candidate
for teaching positions—or the deaconate itself.
Should you want to pursue
the latter vocation, and your age disqualifies you,
a request for a waiver could be granted
by Cardinal Sean O'Malley,
Archbishop of Boston.
It would be worth a try!
And then there is the real estate business.
You already have the broker's license
and need only to upgrade your knowledge
by completing a short
and readily available refresher course.
Of course there are many other possibilities
and opportunities that you may want to explore.
In any case you have my love and best wishes.
I hope that you will keep me posted
on your well-being and activities—
and visit me whenever you can.
You are always welcome at the Cape.

Haiku for Frank D.

An ally is a boon
A good friend is a blessing
An old friend is rare

Love is not earned
It's given by another
Accept it as is

For Kevin and Brian's 62ⁿᵈ Birthday

So, another year has passed
and my twin sons, although aged 62,
have retained their youthful savoir-faire with class.
For Kevin, it was an auspicious year
with many dramatic changes
and several fond but tearful adieus.
For Brian, the year was equally momentous
with business transmutations
personal permutations, and a budding family addition.
* * *
The year 2010 marked the demise
of the long-running Tracey Edwards Company,
the renowned, highly successful,
marketing, branding, and advertising corporation;
the sale of his favorite possession,
a twin-engine, pressurized, and well appointed
Piper Mojave corporate aircraft;
and the loss of his favorite toy,
a 48-foot sleek and luxurious sailboat,
the *Rhapsodie en Bleu.*
It also marked the birth of
Kevin Tracey Companies, LLC,
a new advertising, marketing, branding,
and social media consulting firm.
based in Manchester, New Hampshire.
* * *
The year was equally eventful for Brian—
with the profitable sale of his software firm, Estorian,
and the steady growth of his popular and lucrative
Ride-the-Ducks-of-Seattle tourist attraction.
The year also marked the purchase

of another yacht, the *Entertainer,*
Gulfstar 60 Mark II,
outfitted with the latest navigational
and sailboat technology
and all of the amenities
demanded by the opulently wealthy.
          *   *   *

From a strictly personal point of view.
for Kevin, the year bracketed
the flowering of the prima terpsichorians,
Kolby and Kaylyn Tracey,
his bright, talented, and lovely daughters,
the sale of his Bedford property,
the construction and occupation
of a new condominium in Manchester,
and his renewed status as an eligible bachelor
And for Brian, 2010 not only traced
the maturation of the love of his senior years,
his first granddaughter Grace,
but also the conception of his second grandchild,
a boy to be named Jack, Ethan, or David
by his daughter, Jackie,
and his son-in-law Matt Munson.
          *   *   *

Kevin and Brian have come a long way
since those eventful early adult years.
Both of them pursued very different careers:
Kevin, music education at the Boston Conservatory,
and Brian, premed studies at Boston University.
Next came an abrupt detour of many years duration.
(also involving Bill Jr., the oldest of my four sons,
and later Sean, the youngest)
with the birth of Tracey Entertainment Associates,
soon replaced by The Prodigy,

a top-notch and highly acclaimed show band.
Its first gig was in Boone, Iowa,
and the group remained on the road
on the East Coast and in the Midwest,
including New York City and
Boston, Canada, and the islands of the Caribbean,
performing at night clubs, amusement parks,
and other live entertainment venues
for the ensuing 15 years.
Often accompanied by their wives,
Sue, Joanne, and Lynda,
they lived an interesting and exciting,
although sometimes a difficult
and nomadic existence.
*   *   *

Ultimately, the Prodigy broke up
and only Brian continued on as an entertainer
for the next three years
billed as the Tracey Brothers Show
—while Kevin launched
his advertising and jingle production studio,
Kevin Tracey Productions in Manchester.
From 1988 to 1990 he made
other important career moves
by serving in successive assignments as
Flight Training Development Manager,
Director, Customer Operations and Flight Training,
Director, Customer Operations, Flight Training,
Fleet Sales, Vice President of Marketing,
and Vice President and Assistant Chairman
for Piper Aircraft Corporation in Vero Beach, Florida.
*   *   *

Meanwhile, Brian pursued his TV Career,
one that took him from Boston to New York,
New Jersey, and ultimately to Seattle, Washington.

His assignments included
Host/Producer, Best of New Hampshire,
Reporter, New England Sunday,
Host/ producer, Best of New England,
Host/producer, Evening Magazine Seattle,
Host, America After Hours NBC,
Host, What's New? NBC
Host, Gimmie Shelter, Discovery Channel.
In 1997, Brian embarked on a new career
by founding and serving as
President/ CEO of Ride the Ducks of Seattle,
a major tourist attraction in the city of Seattle.
and establishing a software company, Estorian,
in 2002 and serving as its President/CEO.
* * *

Important elements of their preparation
for successful careers
were the many part time jobs
they held in their teen years—
ranging in difficulty and dedicated commitment
from chicken poop shoveling
at a Townsend chicken farm
and dishwashing at the Old Mill Restaurant
in Westminister,
for Brian;
busboy and dishwasher at the Roncheon Inn
in West Townsend
and soda jerk at the Townsend drug store for Kevin;
and multiple music-related and life-saving
stints for both,
which must be the subject of a new verse
at another time.
* * *

I am very proud of my sons!

They are not only accomplished musicians,
performers, and entrepreneurs,
but they are also exemplary
fathers, sons, brothers, uncles, and friends
to countless men, women,
and children in many locales
going back many years.
HAPPY BIRTHDAY!

Haiku for Kevin and Brian

A man's fantasy
A seductive young woman
In his bed with him

Love is never earned
It's given by another
Accept it as is

A sad misnomer
The infamous "good old days"
So, lighten up guys!

In the business world
Survival of the fittest
Is today's end game

A great rarity—
An understanding woman—
And a gift from God

For Sean and Leah

I don't know how or when you met.
No matter, it was a fortuitous happening!
You were lucky to find each other,
even if your paths crossed only by chance.
And now your lives are intertwined in a relationship
that can only be described as a beautiful romance.
I can even picture what may have happened:
A chance meeting became a smile,
became a conversation,
became a touch,
became a kiss,
became love,
became a destiny,
became a commitment.
And now you are engaged to be married.
I could not be happier for you
—and for me, too,
because I will soon be gaining
a beautiful and loving
granddaughter-in-law—
a perfect match for my handsome and loving grandson.
CONGRATULATIONS and BEST WISHES

For Victor on His 11ᵗʰ Birthday

Today marks another year
of your growth and development
as a happy, talented, and loving young man.
You are a joy to be with
and a gift to observe as you mature.
Here are some thoughts to guide you
in your future endeavors—
and a prayer to protect you
on your journey to adulthood.
*   *   *

Remember, whatever happens,
happens for a reason.
Words can actually hurt much more
than the proverbial "sticks and stones."
Experience is something you don't get
until after you need it.
Set one goal each day
and then work hard to achieve it.
One thing you can always give
and keep is your word.
Of all the things we wear,
our facial expression is the most important.
Life may change us,
but the most important constant is family.

Haiku for Victor

Past the three-point mark
Jumping and launching the ball
End: Nothing but net.

For Leah

Although I do not yet know you well enough,
I have observed you often enough
at family gatherings
to know that my grandson has chosen
his mate wisely.
So, despite a shortage of observational data,
I am taking the liberty of reporting
what I believe to be true about you—
trusting that you will not be offended
by my temerity and candor,
but accepting this snapshot of you
taken by an old man with a practiced eye
for grace. beauty, temperament, and character.
You are woman of exceptional beauty and charm,
and the owner of a repertoire
of personal traits that disarm.
Ever a graceful presence, considerate
and without compare,
with a flair for making others comfortable,
even debonair.
Blessed with a lady-like demeanor,
with sweetness her weapon of choice,
along with an astute ability to socialize with grace.
So, here are my prayers and wishes for you:
May your mornings bring joy
and your evenings bring peace.
May your troubles be few as your blessings increase.
May your special day be full,
your life be long, and your days as sweet
as an Irish song.
HAPPY BIRTHDAY!

For Maura on Her Birthday

Your are a remarkable woman in many ways—
talented, caring, accomplished, regardless of venue—
whether housekeeping, cooking, assembling, repairing,
organizing, employing your people skills—
name it, and you can do it and do it well!
And that includes tasks that are traditionally done by men.

I have enjoyed having you live with me.
Of course, that includes your cooking and cleaning
and taking care of things and me.
But I shall also miss your companionship
and sharing opinions and ideas,
more than anything else.

I have known for many months
that you would be returning to Rome.
What is more important is that I also knew
that it was the right thing for you and Steve—
as well as for Laine and your many friends.
Your heart has always been in Rome, New York,
where it truly belongs—
with your love, your new job, and your friends.

Know, too, that you, Steve, and Laine are welcome
to come to the Cape whenever you can visit.
I hope that there will be more than a few more years
that such trips will be possible.
I look forward to those visits
and will do the best I can to make them happen.
HAPPY BIRTHDAY!

Haiku for Maura

When you love someone
You are blessed beyond belief
When love is returned

-46-

Twins

There are TWO things in life
for which parents are never prepared—TWINS—
although one in every 50 Americans is a twin,
and one in three is an identical twin.
The Tracey family was blessed with a set—
which, in their early years.
elicited the usual dumb questions:
Are they identical?
Which one is older?
Which is the "good" one?
How do you tell them apart?
Do you plan to dress them alike?
And in later years
people displayed skepticism
about their twinship:
Why don't they look exactly alike?
Why do they act differently?
Why do they have dissimilar personalities?
The answers to those questions
require more time than we have.
Suffice it to say that they:
Have identical DNA
Developed a close bond that exists to this day
with daily contact at least by phone
from Washington State to New Hampshire
using their special language
understood by no one else.
And, of course,
they required two of everything
including diapers, bottles,
cribs, carriages, toys,
attention, hugging, and love.

A Tribute to My Brother Frank

Precocious from birth and burgeoning thereafter
Blessed with abundant and formidable talents
And an insatiable appetite for challenge and learning.
Preferring livable houses and quality
but unostentatious vehicles,
appliances, tools, devices, apparel, and accouterments.
A shopper par excellence—numero uno!
That was FX.

An expert salesman and marketer
With a love of "closing the deal."
An accomplished tennis aficionado,
with a Massachusetts Junior Championship Trophy
to prove it.
An avid golfer with a believably low handicap.
(He beat me regularly.)
A formidable opponent in confrontational situations.
That was FX.

Never profane or blasphemous.
Under no circumstances irreverent or impious.
Typically predictable and invariably dependable.
Relentlessly thoughtful and unfailingly authentic,.
Prudent and serious, but accessible and open.
An earnest and successful protector of young Jack.
That was FX.

In other domains, he was genuinely gifted,
and again with a prodigious repertoire of skills:
A sagacious marketer of top-of-the-line products,
a determined and winning representative

of Mr. Donut in Japan and S.S. Pierce and Hall-Smith
Company in the Boston area.
That was FX.

Here is the other side of Francis X, the family man:
A man for whom his Mom, Dad, Wife. Siblings,
Children, and Grandchildren have always been proud.
A caring and devoted husband to Peg
and a doting and adoring father to Kathy and Karen.
A devoted and faithful father to Jim and Mark,
godfather to Kevin (O'Neill) Tracey,
and a loving and warmhearted grandfather to
Deborah and Sandra, Connor and Camden,
and Kristin and Kelli.
That was FX.

But, to all who really knew, respected,
and loved him,
he was more than a faithful family man
and a talented and successful businessman.
He was a much-loved son, husband, father,
brother, grandfather, uncle, and friend—
One who was always supportive and helpful,
a warm and effective advocate and protector,
and a generous benefactor to all
with whom he came in contact.
After God made FX, He destroyed the mold.
May he rest in peace.

Haiku for Frank O.

A wonderful man
That describes F.X. O'Neill
My brother and friend

For Kolby on Her 10ᵗʰ Birthday

The essence of cuteness,
the apple of her Daddy's eye.
the pearl in her Poppi's jewel box,
Kolby is more than a pretty girl—
she is my loving young granddaughter
who is fast becoming a lovely young lady.
So, another year has passed
and Kolby's talents and beauty
continue to develop unsurpassed.
Added to those sterling qualities are
her bright mind and sweet disposition.
She's a blessing to all who appreciate
a first-class lass—
especially her Poppi
who admired and loved her
all the days and years that have passed.
He's so proud of his granddaughter, Kolby.
Her sweet and decorous demeanor
is a wonder to see.
She is a model of perspicacity.
Here is a special Irish prayer
for my lovely offspring:
May God in His Wisdom
and infinite love
look down on her always
from Heaven above.
May He send her good fortune
contentment, and peace.
And may all of her blessings
forever increase.

For Sean T. on His 49th Birthday

This is one of the many occasions
when I need to find and use the words
that will clearly and accurately convey
my heartfelt and profound thoughts and feelings.
But again, the right words seem to escape me.
I feel inadequate about expressing my gratitude
for one of the six greatest blessings I have received
—Sean Michael, my youngest son.
I am indebted to God and to the love of my life,
my wife and his mother, Kathleen,
for that gift, one that has become even more precious
in the years following her untimely death.
I have been privileged to see
Sean's early promise so clearly foretold
by his musical and academic honors
and accomplishments in elementary school,
high school, and college
and his notable and conspicuous success
as an entrepreneur, creative marketer,
and inspirational documentary filmmaker.
Equally impressive, and even more consequential,
are Sean's peerless selection
of the mother of his children
and fulfillment of the crucial
roles of loving husband, father, and role model.
—for an extraordinary wife and mother,
and two bright, caring, and well-disciplined children.
Sean has many years to achieve his goals
I wish that I could be here
to applaud the fruition of Sean's dreams.
I won't, but I'll be watching
and cheering him from the "other side."

For Sean L. on His 32nd Birthday

From the day of your birth,
your Nanni knew that you were someone special.
She loved you unconditionally
and with her whole heart and soul.
The days, months, and years since 1978
have proved that she was right.

You are truly exceptional because:
You are characteristically approachable.
You are unfailingly optimistic
You are habitually considerate.
You are routinely supportive.
You are persistently straightforward,
You are relentlessly honest.
You are consistently hardworking.
You are routinely trustworthy
You are reliably loyal
You are unswervingly kindhearted.
You are unvaryingly considerate.
You are abidingly loving.

To your grandfather, your Poppi.
you are an authentic gentleman—
a man whom he both admires and loves.
HAPPY BIRTHDAY!

Haiku for Sean L.

When you love someone
You are blessed beyond belief
When love is returned

For Victor on His 10th Birthday

Today is your birthday!
It's an auspicious day for you,
but it is special for me, too,
because another year has passed
and your accomplishments continue unsurpassed.

Added to your sterling qualities are
your bright mind and charming disposition.
You're a blessing to all who appreciate
a chap first-class—
especially your Abuelo who admires and loves you
for all of the days, hours, and minutes passed.
Every time we're together,
which is not often enough for me
(I know that time and distance, get in the way)
I discover something else that delights me
about my grandson, Victor.
First and foremost are your God-given talents,
gifts that complement your out-going personality.
Second is the fact that you will carry on
both the Carrillo and Tracey names
with honor and noteworthy deeds.
You are one of only three progeny,
the youngest among William R. III, Timothy and you
to carry the Tracey-O'Neill heritage and bloodline
into the next generation and the world to come.
So, here are a special prayer and a wish for you:
May you always see God's Light on the path ahead.
May troubles never turn your heart to stone,
And may you always remember
when shadows fall you do not walk alone.
HAPPY BIRTDAY!

For Laine on Her 24th Birthday

So, another "big day" has arrived!
I hope that many more significant days are due
for you and whomever else you choose.
Meanwhile, here is my birthday wish for you.
I pray that on this special day,
your heart will be touched in a wonderful way,
that the power of God from above
will bless your life and keep it filled with love.
I pray that you're given special care
so that you'll know someone's always there.
I pray too that you feel everyone's regard for you
in all you ever say, think, believe, or do.
For someone as lovely, charming, and brilliant as you,
I'm hoping you're given good health and satisfaction,
and I'm sure that will happen sooner than anon.
so for your Happy Birthday I ask this today, Amen.
I send this missive with an Irish blessing:
May God in His Wisdom and infinite love
look down on you always from Heaven above.
May He send you good fortune, and peace,
and that all of your blessings forever increase.

For Siara, Writer/Editor

Siara, you may not understand
some of these words.
But, if you keep this verse
until you are only a very few yeas older,
they will mean something that I hope
will be important to you.
* * *
On my Federal and State Income Tax Returns.
I have long identified my principal occupation
as a Writer/Editor.
Never dreaming that one day
I would have a granddaughter
who, very early in life, would earn that title,
I am bounteously blessed.
That *nom de plume* is truly an honorific,
not just a moniker,
because it is acquired only
by the expenditure of large amounts
of time, effort, determination, imagination,
creativity, persistence, and drive—
and not simply the exercise of God-given
talent and potential.
So, I am pleased and profoundly proud
of my granddaughter.
Siara Carrillo Tracey, Writer/Editor
of *Little News* for the 2010-2011 school year.
* * *
This Irish blessing and prayer say
what is in my heart for you.
May the friendships you make,
be those that endure,

and all your gray clouds be small ones for sure.
Trusting in Him to whom we all pray,
may a song fill your heart,
every step of the way.
May you live a long life
full of gladness and health
with a pocket full of gold
as the least of your wealth,
May the dreams you hold dearest,
be those that come true,
And the love that you spread,
keep returning to you.

    *   *   *

Heavenly Father,
I praise you for your gifts to me on this day
and in a grateful way,
I thank you for Siara Carrillo Tracey,
who is very special to her Abuelo/Poppi.

Haiku for Siara

Sun shining brightly
Waves breaking serially
Seagulls complaining

Seeing her is great
Being with her is better
Then I am happy

Loving is a gift
Receiving love a blessing
I am so grateful

For Laine

Today marks another year
of your development
as a happy, talented, lovely,
and loving young lady.
Never doubt for a moment
how much it has meant to me,
to have you as a granddaughter.
There's a special sort of feeling
that's warm and loving, too.
a special kind of pride,
that comes with every thought of you.
Whatever makes you sad
and whatever makes you glad,
to your Poppi matter greatly.
I hope and pray nightly
that many happy days are to come for you.
And always remember this:
Even when words are not spoken,
my love for you is always in my heart.
So, these thoughts on your birthday
are full of hugs for you
to let you know how much you're loved
all year through.
Here is an old Irish prayer:
Dear Father in Heaven
Bless Laine, and surround her with Your love.
Teach her always to follow in your footsteps
and to live her life in the ways of love.
faith, hope, and charity. Amen.
HAPPY 25th BIRTHDAY!

For Grace on Her 3rd Birthday

It has been such a long time
since I last saw you in person,
And held you in my arms.
I miss you,
but I have seen your photos.
You are a lovely little lady!
Do you know that you have
someone in Heaven who loves you
completely and unconditionally?
Her name is Kathleen,
my wife and your Great Grand Nanni.
She was a beautiful, funny,
and loving lady!
Although you were born long after
she had gone to Heaven,
she knows you, and your cousins—
four of her 12 grandchildren
and two great grandchildren
who were born after she left us.
How she would have enjoyed
rocking and singing to you

when you were a baby
and playing with you now!
Those were wonderful times
that she and you missed.
But she has been watching over you
and protecting you
since you were born—
and she will continue to do that
for the rest of your life.
Your Great Nanni also left
some permanent records
with your Daddy for you—
Remembering . . . . the story of her life
on CDs and in book form,
even a VCR of our wedding—
as well as my memories of her in the poems
I have written for her over the years—
and included in my books of poetry,
Strands of Memory and *Strands of Memory Revisited.*
So, ask your Great Grand Nanni,
for her help when you need it—
as your Dad, uncles, aunts, cousins, friends,
and your Poppi do so often.

On Sean and Leah's Wedding Day

Today is the second most important day of your lives.
The day of your birth was the first.
You don't even remember that historic event.
However, you'll always remember this day—Guaranteed!
It marks the beginning of your new life,
a life you fully share for the first time
with any other human being.
For today, you have given each other the greatest gift
that anyone can give to another—
total love and commitment of mind, body, and soul,
now and forevermore.

Your family, relatives, and friends rejoice with you
on this most auspicious of all days,
and wish for you henceforth,
every blessing that God and your loved ones
can bestow—
among them, long and productive lives,
fitness and vitality, joy and happiness,
and everything else that will be useful
to you in God's plan.

And here is another heartfelt wish for you.
My hope and prayer is that you have children—
loving, healthy, and happy children,
if that is God's plan and your wish,
because that, in my own experience,
is the greatest gift of all.

God love you both, this day and always,
Love and felicitations.

For Lina on Her Birthday

Here are my wishes for you on your special day:
Sunshine and a rainbow after spring showers;
Many kisses, hugs, and smiles
and scores of wonderful, happy hours;
flowers at your door, good fortune and laughter, too;
new friendships to warm your heart
and old friendships that never end,
every day your whole life through.
Wishing you a day of extraordinary miracles;
a day full of things to delight in;
a day in which everything is perfect;
a day of knowing that you're someone special;
a day of tranquility, happiness, and joy.
Wishing that you hold tightly
to your best memories for comfort;
and that you thank God for giving you
a devoted, affectionate, and caring husband,
and beautiful, talented, bright, and loving children.
And remember always how much you are loved
so much by so many people in your life.
These words are filled with thoughts,
understanding, and more than anything else,
with hope and earnest prayers that every day ahead
will continue to bring you a large measure of love
and days filled with wishes come true.

Haiku for Lina
A charming woman
Is a priceless gift from God
For men in great need

For Kathy

I'm celebrating your birthday today
for the sunshine you bring
and the warmth that you show.
You brighten every room you enter
as well as every part of my world.
You should know how special you are,
not only to Dennis, Tamra, Sean, and Kaila,
but also to me,
You are so understanding, caring, and forgiving.
That, even knowing all about me,
my positives and my failings,
you show your love for me anyway.
So, this special wish on your birthday
is filled with hugs for you
to let you know how much you're loved
all the year through.
You should also know:
How blessed I am,
how fortunate I've been
that you are my daughter
and also my friend!

For Joanne on Her Birthday

This little verse is for a very special person
who came into my life on the arm
and in the heart of Brian, one of my sons.
She was beautiful and apparently subdued,
a characteristic that would lead one to conclude
that profanity and vituperation
would never pass her lips.
But as she matured she became a mistress
of fulmination
akin to a sailor in the middle of a confrontation.
But she articulated that invective
with charm and captivation.
So, that is Joanne, a bewitching
and beguiling woman—
a favorite daughter-in-law
by my own acclamation.
So, here is my birthday wish for her.
I pray that on this special day,
her heart will be touched in a beautiful way,
that the power from Heaven above
will bless her life and fill it with love.
I pray that she's given special care
so that she'll know someone is always there.
I pray too that she feels everyone's love
in all she ever says, thinks, believes, or does
For someone as lovely, charming,
and amiable as Joanne,
I'm hoping she's granted good health
and much satisfaction,
and I'm sure that will happen sooner than anon.
So for her Happy Birthday I ask this today, Amen.

For Sean L on His 31ˢᵗ Birthday

Today is another special day
for you and for me.
So, here are a few thoughts.
Whether they are true gems or not
is really up to thee.
Every man has to face his demons,
exploit his strengths,
come to grips with his failings,
and accept love in his life.
It's sometimes better to ask forgiveness
than to ask permission.
A true friend is someone
who reaches for your hand
and touches your heart.
To the world you may be one person,
but to one person you may be the world.
The sooner you fall behind,
the more time you'll need to catch up.
It's often far better not to say
what you really think.
because words can actually hurt more
than sticks and stones.
Falling in love is a lot easier
than staying in love.
Understanding how someone else feels
is pretty much impossible.
May the dreams you hold dearest,
Be those which come true,
The love that you spread,
Keep returning to you.
And always remember:
Whatever happens, happens for a reason.

For Mikie on Her 29th Birthday

So, another "big day" has arrived!
However, I sincerely hope
that many more significant days are to come
for you and whomever else you choose.
In the meantime, here is my birthday wish for you.
I pray that on this special day,
your heart will be touched in a beautiful way,
that the power from heaven above
will bless your life and fill it with love.
I pray that you're given special care
so that you'll know someone's always there.
I pray too that you feel everyone's regard for you
in all you ever say, think, believe, or do.
For someone as lovely, charming, and amiable as you,
I'm hoping you're granted good health and much satisfaction,
and I'm sure that will happen sooner than anon.
so for your Happy Birthday I ask this today,
Amen.
Haiku for Mikie
A lovely woman
Always a work of God's art
Let us be thankful

For Siara

My heart is overflowing with love this special day.
My emotions are so strong that I cannot say
all of the things that should be in this essay
to make it a special and memorable bouquet
for my Granddaughter, Siara,
to remember every day.

So, I'm celebrating Siara today
for the sunshine she brings
and the warmth that she emits.
She is the essence of cuteness,
the apple of her Daddy's eye,
the treasure in her Mommy's heart,
and the pearl in her Abuelo's jewel box.
She brightens my world.

Whatever makes her sad,
whatever makes her glad,
to her Abuelo matter greatly.
I hope and pray nightly
that many happy days are to come
for Siara, her brother, Victor,
her Mommy, Lina, her Daddy, Sean,
and whomever else she chooses.

Here is a special Irish wish for you:
May the dreams you hold dearest,
be those which come true,
and the love that you spread,
keep returning to you.

For Tamra on Her 34th Birthday

I remember well the little girl
with the big eyes,
standing in front of my chair
and looking up at me
as if I were something mesmerizing.
When she climbed into my lap,
I was completely captivated,—
fair-haired and fair-skinned,
a diminutive and lovely little lady.
She was my first granddaughter—
the essence of cuteness,
the apple of her father's eye.
the pearl in her mother's jewel box,
and the one who held the first place
in her Poppi's heart.
Here is my message for you during
this trying time:
When disappointment fills your heart,
an employment setback consumes
your soul,
and when doubt invades your mind,
count your many blessings,
especially God's gift of Kaila,
And hopefully you'll find
that even when your heart aches,
God's hand is on your life.
He walks with you in good times,
He carries you through strife.
knowing that this time is stressful
So, I pray for you every night
And I hope that you'll remember
That God can make things right.

For Kaila on Her 3rd Birthday

Because of you, the first of a new generation,
I now know what real love
for a great grandchild can mean.
And that's about as lucky
as an old man can be.
I count myself blessed
to have you to love.
There's a special sort of feeling
That is warm and loving, too,
a special kind of pride
that comes with every thought of you.
You may not understand these words,
although it would not surprise me if you do,
because you are the brightest little girl
that it has been my pleasure to know and view.
So, I offer an Irish blessing for you:
May you be blessed always with
a sunbeam to warm you
a moonbeam to charm you,
and a sheltering angel
so nothing can harm you.

For Kaylyn on Her 11ᵗʰ Birthday

Today is another special day
for you. your Mom and Dad,
your sister Kolby, and for me, too.
So, here are a few thoughts.
Whether they are true gems or not
is really up to you.
* * *

Never doubt how much it has meant to me
to have you as a granddaughter.
There's a special sort of feeling
that's warm and loving, too.
a special kind of pride,
that comes with thoughts of you.
Whatever makes you sad,
whatever makes you glad,
to your Poppi matter greatly.
I hope and pray nightly
that many happy days are to come
for you and whomever else you choose.
And always remember this:
Even when words are not spoken,
my love for you is always in my heart.
So, these thoughts on your birthday
are full of hugs for youto let you know how
much you're loved all year through.
* * *

May the dreams you hold dearest,
be those that come true, and the love that you give,
keep returning to you—and always remember:
Whatever happens,
regardless of the season, happens for a reason.
HAPPY BIRTHDAY!

For Lina on Her 43rd Birthday

This gift of verse on your birthday is unique
because it represents a labor of love
and efforts well spent.
Written for a daughter-in-law I hold dear,
it arrives only once each birthday year.
In celebratory fashion this gift imparts
a loving tradition that comes from my heart.
I have previously and often voiced your praises
as a marvelous wife and mother.
I repeat that assessment here.
So, Lina, this missive is about you.
Sean made a brilliant choice of a woman
to become the mother of his children.
Victor and Siara are blessed,
not only with exceptional talents,
but also with a fabulous mom.
May you always have a shield against hazards,
Laughter to cheer you and brighten your day,
Family and friends you love near you,
And everything else that your heart may desire.
to delight and charm you.

For LB on His 21st Birthday

So, the BIG birthday has arrived!
It marks the legal beginning of your adult life.
I sincerely hope that it also brings some good events
during some of the best years of your young life.
I pray that on this special day,
God will touch your heart in a beautiful way.
I pray that His power from Heaven above
will bless your life and fill it with love.
I pray that He grants you special care
so that you'll know that He's always there.
I pray too that you feel His love for you
in all you ever say, think, believe, or do.
For someone as special as you,
now facing some decisions about your future,
along with your Mom and Dad, I'm sure.
May your blessings outnumber
the shamrocks that grow.
And may trouble avoid you wherever you go.
Hoping God grants you good health and much dough.
I know He'll do that sooner than "then."
So for your Happy Birthday I ask this today, Amen.

For Maura on Her 54th Birthday

My heart is overflowing with love this special day.
My emotions are so strong that I cannot say
all of the things that should be in this essay
to make it a special and memorable bouquet
for my Maura to remember every single day.
However, I sincerely hope
that many happy days are to come
for you, Laine, and whomever else you choose.
In the meantime, here is my birthday wish for you.
I pray that on this special day,
your heart will be touched in a beautiful way,
that the power from heaven above
will bless your life and fill it with love.
I pray that you're given special care
so that you'll know someone's always there.
I pray too that you feel everyone's love for you
in all you ever say, think, believe, or do.
For someone as lovely, charming, and amiable as you,
I'm hoping you're granted good health and happiness,
and I'm sure that will happen sooner than anon.
So for your Happy Birthday I ask this today, Amen.

For Joanne on Her Birthday II

Where have you been?
What have you been up to
—beyond doting on your beautiful granddaughter?
(Remember, that she belongs to me, too).
And, despite your promises, no visits to the Cape
to enjoy my famous hors d'oeuvres,
baked stuffed bay scallops,
and delicious and succulent entrées
I feel neglected: No salty language.
No trash talk. No insults.
However, I'll forgive you,
if you change your ways and get your butt
into an airplane and visit me before it's too late.
Nevertheless, I have this wish for you:
May you be forty years in Heaven,
B'fore the devil knows you're dead.
And, on a more appropriate note:
How blessed I am, how fortunate I've been
that you are my daughter-in-law
and also my friend!
HAPPY BIRTHDAY!

My Sons, The Entertainers

The houselights dim, the snares roll,
and through the loudspeakers
the hushed audience hears,
"Ladies and Gentlemen,
the management is proud to present,
The Tracey Brothers."
The backup band starts up-tempo,
the spots focus on the top of a stairway.
and there they are, four young men
dressed in white from head to toe.
They move down the stairs and on stage,
accompanied by enthusiastic applause,
They pick up their microphones
and begin to sing—
and later dance and play music
from barbershop to bluegrass,
the'30s to the Top 40, ballads to funky,
big band sounds of the '40s,
rock and roll of the '50s,
and the songs and instrumentals
of the '60s and '70s.
I'm in the audience, feeling like laughing
and crying at the same time.
I'm both happy and sad,
"My son, the doctor . . . .
My son, the lawyer . . .
My son, the professor . . .
My son, the architect . . ."
None of those apply.
For me, it's "My sons the entertainers."
Like most young fathers,
my vision of the future

consisted of conventional aspirations
for my boys.
At first, considering their college majors—
business administration, music education,
biology, and philosophy—
it appeared that my forecast
would be fulfilled.
But. it wasn't, and for a variety of reasons,
all of them completely valid.
The fundamental question is this:
Why did my sons, well on the way
to comfortable and rewarding professions,
choose the difficult, arduous,
and demanding profession of
on-stage and TV performers—
and remain entertainers for more than 15 years?
I have my own explanation,
But it is only conjecture, my perception
of what happened.
Unquestionably, the best way to get answers
is to ask the ones who made that choice:
Bill Jr., Kevin, Brian, and Sean.
The next time you see one of them, ask him.
But, I was happy with their choice
because they found what they really
wanted to do with their lives,
at least at that time.
And it s gratifying to know
that their performing careers had value for people,
that they were very good at what they did,
that they achieved a remarkable degree of success at it,
and that they were happy with their careers.
I was and am very proud of my sons.
The Entertainers.

For Kathy on Her 60th Birthday

This gift of verse on your birthday is unique
in the way that it represents a labor of love
and efforts well spent.
Prepared, as a small effort,
for a daughter I hold dear,
it arrives only once each birthday year.
In celebratory fashion this gift imparts
a loving tradition that comes from my heart.
This is the year you retire
from your long and stellar career
as a master teacher, loved by your pupils,
admired by your colleagues,
emulated by your mentees and student teachers,
and respected and appreciated by parents.
My pride in you overflows!
Soon you wont have to face the long drives
early in the morning and late in the afternoon
or evening from Hollis to Ashburnham a
and return in pouring rain, driving snow, numbing cold,
or oppressive heat to teach, mentor,
engage in professional growth, and consult with parents.
Theoretically you will have more time for yourself,
But I know that much of that time
will be lovingly spent with Kaila—
and in good time with your next grandchild.
I close with this birthday prayer:
Heavenly Father, I thank you for Your gifts to me
on this day and in a grateful way,
I thank you for my daughter Kathy
who is very special to her Daddy.

For Kaylyn on Her Ninth Birthday

Today is another special day
for you and also for me.
Whatever makes you sad,
and whatever makes you glad
are very important to your Poppi.
So, here are a few thoughts.
I have been keeping for almost a century
Whether they are true gems or not
is really up to thee.
Nevertheless,
I'm sure that you will understand them
because you are a very smart little lady.
*   *   *

Saying "I love you,"
although nice to hear,
is no substitute for actions
that show that love.
To the world you may be one person,
but to more than one person you are the world.
Words can actually hurt more
than sticks and stones.
Understanding how someone else feels
is pretty much impossible.
When you're feeling very bad or very good,
the feeling doesn't last very long.
*   *   *

Always remember:
A hug is the best gift of all
because one size fits all;
and that whatever happens,
happens for a reason.

For Jackie L.

What is a goddaughter?
She is a lovely little girl child
given in love by her parents
to relatives or close friends
as substitute parents who stand in the wings,
ready and willing to assume that critical role
should a catastrophe to the natural parents occur.
Kathleen and I were honored
in June of 1955 to accept the invitation
of our close friends, Jim and Janet, to so serve.
Thankfully for all, the disaster never occurred.
Although the lives of both families
included many changes,
in terms of physical location, family size,
and the exigencies of life,
we remained close friends,
watching with great pride and love
the development of our godchild
through her childhood, adolescence,
and young adulthood, her nursing career,
and culminating in her beautiful wedding to Scott.
Now, Kathleen has gone home to God in Heaven,
where Jackie now has a special angel
watching over her special godchild
—as well as an aging godfather
who prays for her every night
*   *   *

Here is my special wish for you:
May the dreams you hold dearest,
be those which come true,
and the love that you spread,
keep returning to you.

For Grace on Her 2nd Birthday

Because of you, the 2nd of a new generation,
I know what love
for a great grandchild can mean.
And that's about as lucky
as an old man can be.
I count myself blessed
to have you to love
as well as a great regret
that you live so far away
that I cannot see you every day.
But there's a special feeling
that, despite the distance,
is warm and loving, too,
a special kind of pride
that comes with every thought of you.
You may not understand these words,
although it would not surprise me
if you do,
because you are a bright little girl
that it has been my pleasure
to meet a few times
and also by photos view.
*   *   *

So, on this special day
I offer an Irish blessing for you:
May you be blessed always
with a sunbeam to warm you
a moonbeam to charm you,
and a sheltering angel
so nothing can harm you.

For Kaila on Her Fifth Birthday

Do you know that you have someone in Heaven
who loves you completely and unconditionally?
Her name is Kathleen, my wife and your Great Nanni.
She was a beautiful, funny, and loving lady!
Although you were born long after she had
gone to Heaven,
she knows you, your cousins Kolby, Kaylyn,
Victor, Siara, Grace, and David
four of her 12 grandchildren and three great grandchildren
who were born after she left us.
How she would have enjoyed rocking
and singing to you
when you were a baby and playing with you now!
Those were wonderful times that both you
and she missed.
But she has been watching over you
and protecting you since you were born.
She will continue to do that for the rest of your life.
Your Great Nanni also left some permanent records
with your mother for you—
Remembering . . . the story of her life on CDs and in a book,
even a VCR of our wedding—
as well as my memories of her in the many poems
I have written for her over the years—
and included in my books of poetry,
Strands of Memory and *Strands of Memory Revisited.*
So, remember your Great Nanni, and ask her
for her help when you need it—
as your mother, uncles, aunts, cousins, many friends,
and your Great Poppi
do so often.

For Mikie on Her 30th Birthday

Today is another special day
for your Mom and Dad, Ben,
Jackie, Grace,
for you. and for me, too.
So, here are a few thoughts.
Whether they are true gems or not
is really up to you.
* * *

Never doubt for a moment
how much it has meant to me
and will always mean to me,
to have you as a granddaughter.
There's a special sort of feeling
That's warm and loving, too.
A special kind of pride,
That comes with every thought of you.
Whatever makes you sad,
whatever makes you glad,
to your Poppi matter greatly.
I hope and pray nightly
that many happy days are to come
for you, those named above,
and whomever else you choose.
* * *

May the dreams you hold dearest,
be those which come true,
and the love that you give,
keep returning to you.
And always remember:
Whatever happens,
regardless of the season,
happens for a reason.

For Sean L on His 33rd Birthday

The year just passed was certainly
a momentous one by any and all measures.
It is memorable because it included your wedding—
a high point in life next in importance to your birthday
and an event that you will remember forever.
I was blessed to be able to be there to witness
that wonderful ceremony and family celebration.
I am happy that you found each other,
for you make a spectacular and loving couple.
I also hope to be here when the next event
in the order of importance in your and Leah's lives,
the birth of your first child,
is announced and celebrated.
Remember: to the world you may be only one person,
but to one person, the one you love and married,
you <u>are</u> the world.
That maxim applies both to you and Leah.
Here is my prayer for you:
May the dreams you hold most important
Be those that come true,
The love that you give,
Keep returning to you.
And always keep in mind that:
Whatever happens, happens for a reason.
HAPPY BIRTHDAY!

Haiku for Sean

Hit it where they ain't
That's the goal of the batter
And the way to win

Friendship

Don't spar with your friend
It's better to be yielding
Than to be correct

Fraulein Else-Marie

Although still grieving for her late husband,
she still carries on with resilience,
this lady of my acquaintance—
someone I have known for many years.
although only through occasional encounters
and those only in non-social settings.

Reserved but brilliant,
she is courage personified,
coming to a new land far from her own
and making the trip all alone.

She is a very bright woman, a very quick read,
one who intuitively senses other's needs.
With a photographic memory
for just about anything she sees or hears,
she recalls and remembers with impressive ease.
Sensible, sensitive. and independent,
She has strongly held beliefs and sentiments,
which she articulates with clarity and effectiveness.

So Elsie-Marie is a woman to be prized.
Although we have only seen each other twice,
I consider myself fortunate to have as a friend
someone so very nice.
Knowing that she's charming,
and the reason for this verse too,
I can't say why I admire her so much,
It's enough to know that I do.

Kindness

Kindness is a gift
nestled in one's heart.
It matures only when used.
So share your kindness
wherever and whenever you can
so that it will be returned in kind.
When someone is needy
that is the time for action.
Help that person with kindness.

For a Close Friend

As you celebrate your birthday,
my thoughts and prayers are with you.
For all the goodness and concern
you've shown to me,
I ask the Lord to bless you
on your birthday
and throughout the year.
You are my very special friend.
May your heart be filled with love
and happiness each and everyday
God bless you!

Take My Hand

Take my hand and help me through
the journey, the challenge of this day.
Guide my thoughts and tell me
what you would have me say.

To a Wonderful Friend

If I had a list of favorite people,
you would rank number one.
That is because you are always there
with help and care, a heart of gold,
and a ready smile to warm my spirit
with every glance in my direction.
Once in a great while,
we are lucky enough to meet someone
who makes us feel so good,
so worthwhile, so important—
someone who understands us
in a way that few people ever could—
someone who's truly happy for us.
A person who, when life is going well,
is always there to listen
when we have something new to share
and invariably is the someone
on whom we can depend
for understanding and support
when things are not so good.
I know this because,
by some happy accident,
I found you and learned
that you are the very embodiment
of true friendship.

Haiku

You are my best friend
Don't underrate that status
It's too important

For Clarence on His 41st Birthday

Today is another special day
for you, your Mom, and Kiana.
So, here are a few thoughts.
Whether they are true gems or not
is really up to you.
*   *   *
To the world you may be one person,
but to one person you may be the world.
Every man has to face his demons,
exploit his strengths,
come to grips with his shortcomings,
and accept love in his life.
It's sometimes better to ask forgiveness
than to ask permission.
Keep your words soft and sweet
just in case you have to eat them.
The sooner you fall behind,
the more time you'll need to catch up.
It's often far better not to say
what you really think,
because words can actually hurt more
than sticks and stones.
The heaviest thing anyone can carry is a grudge.
Understanding how someone else feels
is pretty much impossible.

Haiku for Clarence

Yesterday is gone
Tomorrow may never come
So live for today

For My Friend Peggy

Friends for more than 60 years,
the bonding of the Traceys and the McDowells
began in 1944 when Kathleen and Peggy
taught together at the Lyman School in Ashby—
while Peggy's husband Paul
was serving in the Army in Iceland
and I was serving in the Navy
in the South Pacific.
Rooming together in Ashby,
Kay and Peg spent many hours
playing contract bridge.

After the war, we began to exchange visits
and celebrate minor holidays together
in Ashby, Ashburnham, Leominster,
Fitchburg, and later, on Cape Cod,
where peg and Paul owned a cottage.
The parties were fun and involved many friends,
all of whom are now gone.

Our son Brian and Peg's son Bobby
became friends and shared time together.
Peg was Brian's godmother.
We had the good fortune to attend each other's
50th anniversary celebrations here on the Cape.
Kay, Paul, and Peg are now deceased.
Although for a few years Peg and I occasionally
met for breakfast when Paul and Kay were gone.

The only things remaining are our children and
my memories of better times.

For My Friend Janet

Mother of sons Jay and Paul
and daughter Jackie, my godchild.
Always upbeat, warm-hearted, and caring,
interested and striking,
yet fun loving and carefree.
Oh, the good times we shared in our salad years,
the parties in Worcester, Northboro, and Ashby,
and, in more recent years, on Cape Cod.
It should be easy to express one's thoughts
about someone who means a great deal to me
because it's simply a matter of saying what you feel.
But, in practice it's not that simple
because the memories are so special
that you want to remember them clear.
But how do you capture the phrases
that say what you feel about a close friend
and her so-special ways?
She was a friend to Kathleen and me
about 45 years—more than 16,000 days.
She accepted us just as we were.
She'd laugh when I was trying to be funny
She helped me when I was hopeless
and cried with me when I was sad.
She's a friend who stood with me
through good times and bad.
She was there for me when Kathleen passed on,
inviting me to cocktails and dinner
in the most trying years for me.
She epitomizes the maxim,
"a friend in need is a friend indeed."

Sheila

Winsome and lithe, dainty and shapely,
with a figure made to be hugged.
Large brown eyes filled with youthful coyness
and Oriental wisdom
looking deeply into your heart and soul
and making judgments about your psyche.
With long black tresses
flowing below her shoulders,
begging to be touched,
surrounding a lovely face, waiting to be kissed.
Owning a friendly persona, warm and kind,
interested and interesting,
yet fun-loving and carefree.
Blessed with a lovely and musical voice
in speech and song, a pleasure to hear.
But her most arresting quality
is her sensitivity to the wants and needs
of those she meets.
So this is my initial reading of Sheila,
based only on infrequent, short meetings.
When and if I know her longer,
I'm certain that I can do better.
Nevertheless, in the meantime, she is to me
a fascinating and intriguing girl-woman,
a model of beauty and femininity.

Haiku for Sheila

Ever a charmer
Always helpful to others
A model to match

For My Friend Bernadette

Mother of five sons, Andre, Paul,
Robert, Thomas, and William,
and the wife of Honore
for more than 50 years,
Bernadette is the epitome
of a disappearing genre of women,
the stay-at-home wife and mother.
Bernie, as she is called, put family
ahead of everything else.

I believe that is an important "ministry"
in our tumultuous and perilous world.
But Bernie has equally engaging attributes.
She cares for people
and invariably shows
warmth and concern
for their welfare.

Bernie has been my and Kay's friend
for more than 50 years
and an across-the-street neighbor
for more than 30 of those years,
We have shared good times and bad,
but the happy times outnumber the sad.

Although we mourn Henry's passing,
for the Camires and Traceys,
the good memories are strong
and will always remain with us.
Acquaintances come and go,
but true friends are with us forever.

For My Friend Janice

She is the mother of my granddaughters
Kolby and Kaylyn.
She is a horsewoman extraordinaire,
a baby-maker without compare,
the apple of her mother's eye,
and Kolby and Kaylyn's lifelong ally.
An e-mail aficionado,
she sends messages that invariably include
jokes to give recipients a chuckle.
A fan and talented tennis personal coach,
and invariably the winner
whenever she competes.
A strong-willed and independent woman,
whatever she starts
she is determined to finish—
and does so with exceptional panache.
A woman with many interests
including music, sports, health,
child rearing, and people,
she is gregarious. affable, hospitable,
and sociable.
A fanatic about good health and nutrition
she practices what she preaches
as her primary mission.
The results of her labor are there
for all to see,
the accomplishments of her children
and her top notch physique.
So that is Janice to have and to hold
a dedicated mother with a heart of gold.

For My Friend Jim

An amiable raconteur and jokester.
Master of the art of mixing very dry martinis
and other adult beverages.
His main claim to fame:
a practical joker without peer.
And, as I must admit,
I was often the victim of his wicked wit.

First, during an evening in his basement playroom,
Jim served me a sandwich laced
with gentian violet pills.
The days that followed were a nightmare.
Standing in front of the urinal
at Fitchburg State the next morning
I was horrified to see
jet black ink pouring from my private package.
During the days that followed,
the "ink" changed color from black
to purple, then to dark blue, green,
and finally to its normal light yellow.
All that time I wondered and worried
what dread disease I had contracted.

The second memorable event
again occurred at Jim's home.
While showing off his beautiful new truck,
with me seated in the passenger seat,
and without any warning,
Jim activated a lever
that caused the cab to tilt forward,
nearly flinging me through the windshield.

The third instance of mischief
was also committed at Jim's home.
Kay and I left his house at about one A.M.,
with me about two sheets to the wind.
Within about one mile of Jim's house,
the engine of my Pontiac station wagon
began to stutter and skip badly.
Fortunately, it did not quit but kept sputtering
during the long trip back to Ashby.
My faith in my old car was confirmed.
The next day I discovered that Jim
had disconnected two of the six spark plugs,
causing us to chug along
for some 40 miles on four cylinders.

.So that's our fun-loving Jim,
our friend for more than 45 years
and still playing his practical jokes,
although not as often.
And we loved him anyway!

Haiku for Jim and Janet!

Master of horseplay
Surprises his stock in trade
Yet a friend to all

Always a lady
Ever mindful of her role
A model for all

Be calm and serene
Change your attitude toward life
By will and prayer

For Sam

To my wife, Kathleen,
Sam was "The Margin Man."
But, he is much more than that.
He is Dad to my granddaughter Laine,
and to Leah and Laurie,
and grandfather to Joel Jr., McKenzie,
Sam, Ryan, and others here on earth—
and to Courtney, a saint in Heaven!
Sam is also a cook in his own right,
an Italian chef who prepares delicious
spaghetti sauce with meatballs and sausages
about every fortnight—
and often shared his bounty with me
on my visits to Rome
much to my stomach's delight.
So, Sam is a man with many talents.
a man for all seasons
and a friend to share a Dewar's scotch
for any, all, or no reasons.

Haiku for Sam

Rubber to home plate
Just sixty feet six inches
Baseball's key metric

In baseball parlance
A pitcher's best redeemer:
Double-play ground ball

Kelley and Katie's Visit

During the period August 11-17 August 2010,
we were graced by the presence of two visitors,
beautiful, well behaved, courteous,
and solicitous young ladies—
one my granddaughter
and the other her lifetime friend.
The weather provided perfect summer days
with sunshine,
temps between low 70s and high 80s,
low humidity except for two days—
and beautiful star-filled nights,
with meteor showers on two of those nights.

If you're fond of sand dunes and salty air
Quaint little villages here and there
You're sure to fall in love with old Cape Cod

Kelley and Katie did see and feel
the beach sand and salty air at Smuggler's
and the Red Jacket beaches,
the Bass and Parker's Rivers,
and the quaint villages of Bass River,
West Yarmouth, and Hyannis.

If you like the taste of a lobster stew
Served by a window with an ocean view
you're sure to fall in love with old Cape Cod,

Although they didn't have lobster stew,
they did enjoy breakfasts of scrambled eggs
and French toast,
snacks of pizza, burgers, and ice cream,

and dinners of Poppi's famous
roast pork loin with mashed potatoes, gravy,
green beans, peas, and whole kernel corn.
(even butternut squash),
and Maura's spaghetti and meatballs.
They also sampled some salt-water taffy!

Winding roads that seem to beckon you
Miles of green beneath a sky of blue
Church bells chimin' on a Sunday morn
Remind you of the town where you were born

They didn't make it to Route 6A.
the "winding road"
from Sandwich to Provincetown.
But they did check out the Saturday nightlife
(chaperoned by Maura) of downtown Hyannis.
Unfortunately, Kelley didn't get a chance
to sing *Jessie's Girl*, at one of the Karaoke cafes,
but both Katie and Kelley did try on
some 20s, 30s. and 40s-style dresses,
which happily emphasized their youthful beauty.
They also played golf at the Pirate's Cove
and the Skull miniature golf courses,
watched several movies on CDs,
and attended a showing of "Dinner for Schmucks"
at the Cape Cod Mall Stadium 12 Regal Cinemas.

If you spend an evening you'll want to stay
Watching the moonlight on Cape Cod Bay
You're sure to fall in love with old Cape Cod

I hope that the evenings they spent
sharing a queen-sized inflatable bed in my office

allowed them to get several nights of sleep.
In any case, they did not complain!
And I truly hope that that they both
fell in love with old Cape Cod.

You are young women
of beauty and charm,
and the owners of a repertoire
of personal traits that disarm.
Ever graceful presences, considerate
and without compare,
with a flair for making
others comfortable, even debonair.
Blessed with lady-like demeanors,
with sweetness their weapon of choice,
along with an astute but quiet ability
to socialize with grace.

Here are my wishes for you:
Sunshine and a rainbow
after spring showers;
Many hugs and smiles
and scores of wonderful, happy hours;
flowers at your door, good fortune
and laughter, too;
new friendships to warm your heart
and old friendships that never end,
every day your whole life through.

Note: Lines in italics are from the popular song,
Old Cape Cod, recorded by Patti Page in 1957.

For Lucille on Her Birthday

Today is an auspicious day for you—
and for your children and grandchildren, too.
Glad to hear that Matthew is back safely from Iraq,
and will marry in June;
that Erin is preparing for a teaching career;
that Sara is following her star in a new venture;
that Marie and Marylou are doing well;
and that Sharon and Harry (and Bella) are giving you
the solicitous support and love
that you so richly deserve.
I am pleased that you are doing what is needed
to improve your health—
and that you remain active in the Senior Center.
But I am saddened to hear that Doris and Bea
are not doing well in their fight
against the ravages of aging.
As for me, despite the vicissitudes of daily living,
I admit to having difficulty believing
that I will soon be 87,
and that it has been more than 60 years
since we last met at the Worcester Auditorium
and danced for the last time.
But, this verse is about you.
Here are my wishes:
May your mornings bring joy
and your evenings bring peace.
May your troubles be few as your blessings increase.
May God give you . . . .
For every storm, a rainbow, for every tear, a smile
For every care, a promise, and a blessing in each trial.

War

War is hell on earth
It destroys people and hope
It gives back nothing

Memories

Memory flashes of ties that bind.
in the treasure-house of the mind,
A stormy sea misbehaves,
screeching winds and mountainous waves,
pitching and rolling our LST
sailing in convoy across dangerous seas.

The bos'n's pipe shrills over the PA,
alerting all hands to the orders of the day.
"Now hear this," for what we're about,
work party, chow down, mail call,
battle stations, "the smoking lamp is out."
"Stand by your station" the order of the day,
and no sailor can afford
to miss inspection with the flotilla
commander aboard.

Standing at attention on the weather deck,
in close-order lines in the uniform of the day,
dress blues, battle greens, or dungaree jeans,
from the galley wafts the aroma of fresh bread.
which will be eaten with canned spam and beans,
and strong coffee from below.

And when in port, such a rare event,
we hear the long awaited order on the PA'
"Last call, all ashore that's going ashore."
Can we ask for more?
From ties that bind so many years ago,
in the treasure-house of the mind.

An Agonizing and Arduous Time

Learning that my oldest son had enlisted
in the Army
Remembering my service in World War II
Hoping that conflict would be the very last War.
Feeling pride that my son was willing to serve.

Visiting him at Fort Gordon, GA
where he was being trained in helicopter repair
and maintenance.
Having responsibility for administering training
for Warrant Officer pilots in ARDF operations
at Forts Devens, MA and Fort Huachuca, AZ,
and for officer, noncommissioned officer,
enlisted personnel, and civilians of all military services
in intelligence and security occupational specialties
at Fort Devens, MA, Pensacola FL,
San Antonio, TX, and Petaluma, CA.
Understanding the dangers associated
with air and other military operations anywhere.

Experiencing concern when my son was assigned
to a chopper unit in Vietnam.
Enduring the long anxious months during
his assignment as a helicopter crew chief.
Sustaining envy when two of my subordinates
were allowed to visit units in Vietnam,
including the one to which my son was assigned.
Continuing resentment when those visitors spent
quality time with my son when he was given
weekend passes for R&R in Saigon.
Discerning my son's ambivalence about his Vietnamese
paramour, Thu, when his 18-month tour was ending.

Empathizing with his feelings about leaving her
in Vietnam or bringing her back to the USA to face the
inevitable discrimination from narrow-minded people.

Awakening early one morning to see my son
trudging up Richardson Drive balancing a bulging
sea bag on his shoulder
and carrying a smaller bag in his other hand.
Experiencing relief and thanksgiving
for his safe return home.
Noting with sadness and anguish
the lack of community, state, and national
celebration and gratitude
to those who fought, were wounded,
and died for their country,
or returning as veterans of an unpopular war.
Unfortunately, inexplicably, and shamefully,
that was the way it happened.

Haiku about War

Vets of World War II
The greatest generation
A breed that's dying

The hallmarks of war
Bedlam, chaos, confusion
Fear and loneliness

Youth of all races,
Sizes, genders, uniforms
Some become heroes

The Uniform

I first wore the uniform of the United States Navy
in July 1943, a few days after reporting
to the Navy V-12 initial officer selection
and training program
at the College of the Holy Cross in Worcester, MA.
The uniform was that of the lowest
enlisted grade possible,
apprentice seaman, often referred to as the "crackerjack"
(because of the Navy-uniformed figure
that adorns the Cracker Jack snack box).

The navy blue dress uniform included
"bell bottom" trousers,
with 13 buttons on the front flap,
a matching jumper with a back-hanging "tar flap" collar,
with three rows of white piping on the collar and cuffs,
a black polyester neckerchief,
and a white sailor cap
(nicknamed the "Dixie cup" after the paper cups).

I wore that uniform until March 1944
when I entered Midshipmen's School
at Colombia University, New York,
I was outfitted with officers' dress blues, dress whites,
service grays, work khakis and grays (with midshipmen's
brass and gold
or black stripes on collars, caps, or shoulder boards),
Upon commissioning in June 1944,
officer brass and stripes
replaced the midshipmen's insignia.
In January 1946,

I continued wearing the navy and khaki service dress
uniforms during reserve duty
until I retired from the Navy in July 1969.

Until my retirement from the US Army Intelligence School,
Fort Devens, MA as a GM 15 in December 1982,
I had worked all of my adult life with
and for uniformed Army soldiers,
Navy sailors, Marines, and Air Force
personnel of all ranks,
from private and seaman E-1,
through sergeant major, E-9,
warrant officers WO1 through CWO4,
and from second lieutenant and ensign O-1
through colonel/captain 0-6 to lieutenant general 0-9.

I was proud to serve many general and flag
officers as a consultant
and on several occasions to brief general officers,
including the Army Chief of Staff
and Assistant Secretaries of the Army and Defence.

I was always proud to wear the uniforms.
knowing full well that the freedoms
we enjoy were originally won and are defended
today by the men and women who wear them.
They volunteered for service in the Armed Forces
and ready to give their lives in service if called to do so
by our country and its citizens.
I was also proud to be married in my Navy uniform
and have arranged to be buried in it
when that time comes.

New Beginnings

When I returned to you, my wife and home,
in January 1946,
every day offered a beginning
because every morning
my world was made new,
and there was so much catching up to do.

Despite relief from the loneliness and sadness
of the years at war,
I still had hope for myself and also for you.
All things of yesterday are past and over,
my military work is done,
our tears have been shed.
Yesterday's mistakes are covered over,
healed by the balm that time has dispersed,
we start our lives anew.

So every day offers a fresh beginning,
allowing our hearts to listen to a joyful refrain.
In spite of bad memories,
we can take heart and begin our lives again.
So, with resolute hearts and true,
let us go forward on our way.
We both have the inner strength to do
the tasks that come our way:
There are university degrees to complete,
professions to learn and practice,
family and children to build and nurture,
and a unique legacy to bequeath,
Let's do it!

Nature

Fight global warming
Replace, reduce, or adjust
To save energy

Cape Cod Spring

Most people of New England enjoy four distinct
seasons—except those who live
on Cape Cod—
where there are only three:
winter, summer, and autumn.
Beautiful spring, exquisite spring,
arrives annually everywhere else—
in Maine, New Hampshire,
Vermont, Massachusetts,
Rhode Island, and Connecticut—
where the sun rises earlier and sets later
every day, crocuses appear, and
birds, including the non-feathered snowbirds,
return from their southern winter vacations.
All except the later do not happen
on Cape Cod,
Instead, it rains (and sometimes snows)
in March, April, and May—
almost every other day is cold, wet, and dreary,
bleak, miserable, and depressing.
However, the spring of 2010 was a remarkable
and most unexpected exception,
Cape Cod, its natives, and wash-ashores
enjoyed an authentic spring.
The returning birds of all persuasions
were treated to warming sunrises, stunning sunsets,
burgeoning landscapes,
arresting seascapes, and just enough soft (Irish) rain
to keep everything
budding, growing, and green.
It was the most magnificent spring
I have experienced in 62 years on Old Cape Cod.

Cape Cod Diversions

Even if you do them only occasionally,
and often unsuccessfully, there are many pastimes
worth the investment of the time they require.
Here are some of my favorites:
Hunting for driftwood, preferably small natural
hard wood flotsam in interesting and unique shapes,
rather than man-made debris, to serve as decorations
or conversation pieces for your home.
Visiting the habitats of ospreys
to watch them from a noninvasive distance,
building or repairing their nests and executing
their spectacular fishing performances.
Prospecting for "mermaid's tears" on the beaches—
searching for stunningly lovely nature-made
sea glass, in various shapes and colors,
formed and polished over time by sand and sea.
Listening closely to the percussion concerts
of woodpeckers as they seek to attract mates
or proclaim their jurisdictions
by their persistent drumming on any available surface.
Watching the antics of seagulls
as they take advantage of every opportunity
to feed themselves,
even by dive-bombing you
to snatch a bite of your hamburger or hot dog,
as you sit on the beach.
And let me not overlook the simple pleasure
of bird-watching, with or without binoculars,
to openly or surreptitiously admire
the strikingly lovely, bikini-clad women
sunbathing, playing beach ball, or swimming
at any of Cape Cod's superb beaches.

Sea Glass

Sharding or glassing, a shore hobby for beachers
—searching for what they call mermaid's tears,
typically in the late summer or early autumn.
Cape Cod glassheads slowly walk the beaches
at low tide after a storm,
heads down with eyes moving slowly from side to side,
and stopping occasionally to kick gently at the sand
or bending over to dig something up
with a hand, a small tool, or a stick.
If lucky, they are rewarded by unearthing
a "cooked" shard of sea glass,
weathered by 30 years or more
of wave action and high water pH
to smooth edges and pit surfaces
and washed onto the beach from deeper waters,.
Or they have been buried on the beach for years,
and uncovered by the action of the tides.
The odds are that they will find either a brown
or green shard, the most common discovery.
If lucky, they will find a more valuable shard.
In order of rarity, from lowest to highest:
blues (cobalt and cornflower or azure),
aqua and seafoam (unique).
purples (due to oxidized manganese in clear glass),
yellows and oranges,
and red, the ultra scarce and truly exceptional treasure.
The value of sea glass varies considerably—
from nothing to $300 or more per shard,
depending on size, shape, color, and weathering.
But to the inveterate, passionate, or ardent collector,
sea glass finds are priceless.
I could be one of those aficionados.

The Osprey

The reigning king of Cape Cod's avian world.
the obstreperous osprey is a large raptor,
one of 400 pairs mated for life statewide,
with 50 pairs nesting on the Cape.
Sometimes known as sea hawks or fish eagles,
ospreys can be spotted on Scusset Marsh,
Mashpee Island, Barnstable Harbor's Great Marsh,
Monomoy National Wildlife Refuge, Nauset Marsh,
Wellfleet Bay Wildlife Sanctuary, and elsewhere
near lakes, streams, estuaries, and marshes.

Ospreys return to the Cape in early spring
to start the serious business of perpetuating the species
—building or repairing nests,
making courtship flights to attract or entertain a mate,
laying eggs, incubating, feeding,
and rearing their fast-growing, ever-hungry young,
Having a wing span of four to six feet,
the male osprey's upper feathers
are a deep, glossy brown,
almost black, the breast is white and sometimes
streaked with brown, and the underparts are pure white.
The head is white with a dark mask across the eyes,
reaching to the sides of the neck.
The bill is black and the feet are white
with black talons.

A short tail and long, narrow wings
with four long, finger-like feathers,
and a shorter fifth, give it a very distinctive look.
The sexes are fairly similar in coloration,
but the adult male can be distinguished from the female

by its slimmer body and narrower wings.
The smaller female, although similarly tinted,
has a larger band of mottling across the breast
and barring on the underwings and tail.

The osprey is an accomplished fisherman.
When he spots a fish from the air,
he hovers at a height of 10 to 30 meters
until the fish is in a catchable position.
Then, in a dramatic performance,
the bird dives from the sky
with his wings half closed, claws stretched forward,
and disappears under the surface
in a great splash of water,
usually reappearing a few seconds later
with a fish firmly clutched in his talons.

After taking off, the Osprey turns the fish
so that its head faces forward
to reduce aerodynamic drag.
He emits piercing, high-pitched calls high in the sky,
while dangling the fish in his talons
as his female companion
flies along beneath enjoying the drama,
The osprey mates head back to the nest
to watch over their young as they feast on the catch.

Haiku
Ospreys building nests
Home for a raptor family
Marvelous to see

Gifts from the Sea

A treat for the palate—
year or two-old oysters on the half-shell,
needing only, if anything at all,
a squeeze of fresh lemon.

But first you have to get the mollusks.
those succulent gifts from the sea.
The easiest, least expensive, and best way to get them
is to buy them fresh from an aquaculture farmer
tending his crops on the flats of Cape Cod,
perhaps the ones off Bone Hill Road in Cummaquid.
There, as in many other shell fishing grants,
sacks full of young oysters
are hanging in their string hammocks.
awaiting the high tide
that will feed, filter, and clean them,
readying them for market.

Make your visit on a
beautiful, cloudless morning in July or August,
when the sun is shining brightly,
the ocean water is a deep turquoise,
low tide has exposed the mud flats,
the songbirds are singing,
and Sandy Neck lighthouse can be seen
in the distance.
The shopping expedition,
and the gastronomic experience that follows
will be well worth your investment
of time and treasure.

Clamming for Steamers
(Soft-shell clams)

After paying high prices many times
for a few dozen clams,
I've discovered that clamming not only saves money,
and provides exercise, but it's also lots of fun.
There's something exceptionally satisfying
about foraging for dinner in the scores of tidal flats
from Barnstable Harbor to Provincetown
on both the bay and the ocean sides of Cape Cod.

You'll need a few things to get started.
First, you must have a permit from town hall.
If you get caught without it, you'll face a stiff fine.
When you're at town hall, check to see
if any areas are closed to shell fishing.
Next you'll need a clam gauge or clam ring.
Just like the permit, you're in big trouble
if you're caught without one.
The local hardware or bait store probably has them.

When you catch a clam,
if it won't pass through the ring the long way,
you're catch is legal.
You must have either a peck or bushel basket
to measure your daily catch.
But if you have a gallon sized bucket,
or something that is a specific measure,
you'll probably be okay.
You just need something to prove
that you're not taking more than the daily limit.

A tide chart will also come in handy—
"Happy as a clam at high tide"—
because nobody can get them when the tide's in.
Many liquor and mom-and-pop convenience stores
have them free at the register.

A clam rake is optional, but it does help.
You can harvest clams with your hands,
but a pair of canvas or leather gloves
will prevent cuts from broken shells.
Any tool that can turn over 10-12 inches of mud is o.k.

The last things you'll need to find are the flats
where the clams are hiding.
That will come primarily from local knowledge.
But, if you look out from shore and see people
on their hands and knees with a bucket,
you're probably at a good clamming spot.
If one of the shellfish police is at town hall
when you get your permit,
he or she would be your best bet for information

When you're out on the flats, look for clam holes,
plunge the rake in about 6 inches above a hole
as deep as it will go,
and pull it toward you to turn over a small mound.
Sift through the mud with your hands,
and. hopefully, you'll find "keeper" clams.

A note of caution:
don't stray far from shore at low tide
and get cut off as the tide comes in.
That could happen on the Cape Cod Bay side
where the tide may rise and fall as many as ten feet.
When you bring your catch home,

you should clean the clams thoroughly.
Soak them in a bucket of water for several hours.
Be sure to change the water frequently,
otherwise, they will use up all the oxygen
in the water and suffocate.
When you're ready to cook the clams,
sprinkle a generous amount of corn meal into the water.
That makes the clams discharge sand.
Don't leave the clams in the corn meal
more than a few hours.
Any floating clams should be discarded.
They're dead.
Throw the clams into a covered pot
with a half-cup of water
and set it on high heat.
As the clams open, they will generate more water.
Steam them for three minutes,
or until the shells are open—and one minute more.
Pass the drawn butter and enjoy!

Haiku

Nature gone berserk:
Hurricanes. floods, tornadoes
Earthquakes and wildfires

A sure sign of spring
Mating tree frogs atrilling
The peepers at work

Human encroachment
Crowding out other species
Result: ravishment

Driftwood

One of the most rewarding hobbies of earlier years,
opportunities for collecting driftwood,
are now few and far between.
The lake and ocean shorelines and beaches
are no longer barren stretches of terrain.
They re either so isolated, so near human habitation,
or parts of state or national parks and preserves
that they are no longer available for foraging.
However, in most area, with the exception of the parks,
a person may gather or collect for personal use,
reasonable quantities of natural products
or renewable nature,
including seashells and driftwood
if not collected for resale.
So, collecting driftwood, usually small bits and pieces,
offers many pleasurable hours
searching, diving, foraging, prospecting, or digging
for items that can be used unchanged
for decorations or cutting, shaping, polishing,
or otherwise modifying them
for functional or practical purposes/
Driftwood floats in on many shorelines worldwide
in two different forms of flotsam and jetsam:
man-made—wood that has been cut into boards
or crafted into other objects,
such as picture frames, furniture, and furnishings
—and nature made—trees. branches, and roots.
Both are the products of storms, hurricanes, typhoons, tsunamis,
floods,
earthquakes, and tidal erosion,
which send houses and other structures out to sea
from island and coastal shores.

Other sources include boats and ships
sunk by storms, broken up, and floated around,
sometimes for years,
and dunnage, wood that has been used
to stabilize cargo
and is dumped off ships at sea
when no longer needed.
In many areas where coastal shores are protected
by marine sanctuaries and national parks.
it may be illegal to remove natural driftwood
since it has become part of the ecosystem.
However, in most areas that receive driftwood
in the form of trash, collecting these materials
is encouraged to clean up the environment.
Wood may drift in the ocean currents
for weeks, months, even years,
and travel many miles around the world
before it comes to land.
During this time at sea the wood is attacked
by Teredo worms, often called ship's worms.
These worms attach themselves as small larvae
and grow in size as they bore into the wood.
Softer woods can be almost completely consumed
in a matter of time, while hardwoods and woods
that reach land sooner are less wormy.
The worms die when the wood dries out
when it's out of the water.
Driftwood is best collected by walking the beach
at low tide.
Here are some tips for collecting driftwood:
Choose wood that is hardwood.
Stay away from pine, cedar, and elm.
Choose dry driftwood if possible.
It can be polished and used immediately,

while wet driftwood must be cleansed and dried.
Weathered unique wood makes a better find
than a chunk of wood.
Wash any debris or bark off the wood.
Boil the wood in water for 2 to 3 hours
to accelerate the process of leeching the tannins out.
It will also sterilize the wood and destroy
any unwanted guests.
Clean driftwood by rinsing it thoroughly
with cold fresh water.
And polish it when it has dried by using
a light-colored polish.
Enjoy nature's bounty!

A Morning Stroll

In the soft dew and early clouds
of a Sunday morn,
I took my morning stroll
a regular route on my usual beach patrol.
Along with me I brought an imaginary friend
because I had a need to converse
with someone who to my prayers attends.
I unburdened my heart and soul
and spoke of many things:
of plans gone wrong, of failure's sting,
of physical afflictions, and emotional distress,
of rejection by a long-time friend,
and how to live with shattered dreams.
My friend listened quietly,
not saying a single word,
For it was His turn to listen
And my turn to be heard.

The Spring and Summer of 2010

Plentiful and gently warming sunshine,
despite the short but ever lengthening days.
Infrequent and totally bearable soft Irish rain.
Bounteous crocuses soon followed by daffodils
and blossoming yellow forsythia,
the "golden bells" that herald the arrival of spring.

It was a truly magnificent
and uncommon Cape Cod spring,
the first one that I can remember
in the last 28 years.
Then came the supreme encore—
an incredible and magnificent summer,
one with day after day of warm sunshine,
temperatures in the mid 70s and 80s,
low humidity most days
with dew points in the mid 60s,
only a few days of oppressive heat and humidity.

Unfortunately lawns and gardens suffered
a need for irrigation due to the infrequent
and short duration of rain.
Nights. however, were also ideal—
idyllic and heavenly, typically cloudless skies.
with a plethora of star constellations
and an abundance of planets shining brightly.

The rare summer weather was a godsend
to those in summer visitor-related businesses
but also to year-round Cape Codders, wash-a-shores,
and the snowbirds who winter in the south.
Let's pray for a repeat performance next year!

Signs of Spring on Cape Cod

It's true that spring on Cape Cod is more
a state of mind than a physical reality.
The vernal equinox on Cape Cod,
the time when the sun crosses the celestial equator
and day and night are of equal length,
marking the beginning of spring,
always occurs.

But all too often, the signs of spring in other locales
are completely missing.
and are replaced by continuing signs of winter—
freezing days and nights, strong winds
and even snow storms on the Cape.
Jackets, hats, gloves. long sleeves, hang around
for another month or so
while we're still looking at a gray landscape.
Yes, there's a little green here and there—
most due to the chemicals placed on lawns—but
tt's true that spring often catches cold on Cape Cod!

Then the annual miracle occurs:
We have an occasional sunny day
When the temperature rises to 70 degrees
or even higher!
What bliss it is to feel the warm sunshine
on my shoulders and smell the fresh salt air.
If nothing else, our long cold winters
make me fully appreciate the warmer weather
when it finally comes.
Yet, despite the lengthening days,
causing clocks to be jumped ahead one hour,

the appearance of crocuses
is often marred by a one or two inch blanket
of snow through which the tender buds
must emerge.
The effect of those impediments,
is the absence of spring many years
and the transition from one season to another
takes the unusual three term sequence
of fall, winter, and summer
with no real spring at all.
Nonetheless, cheerful white, violet purple,
and yellow, crocus blossoms
provide the exclamation points
at the end of a cold winter.
Hurrah for the crocuses!

The Evening Sky

Shadow beauties
outline God's evening sky.
Mountains in their majesty,
peaks pointing high.
Multiform rooflines
on the houses, sheds, and barns
that dot the hills and vales
with picturesque country charm.
Oak and maple trees towering
in perfect symmetrical form,
Upward-reaching chimneys
that proclaim home and warmth.
Trees with leafless branches
of intricate and enigmatic design.
What shadowy beauties
outline God's evening sky.

The Noisy Woodpeckers

No, I don't have holes on the exterior of my house'
although the woodpeckers have been busy
with early spring mapping of their territories.
My house is protected by vinyl siding and windows
and aluminum gutters and window trim boards,
So, along with the metal flashing
around plumbing vents and the chimney cap,
the birds have plenty of targets
for their incessant drumming—
the rapid staccato of beaks
meeting vinyl, aluminum, and metal
instead of their preference for pecking on wood.
Tree trunks and other sources of wood
are the usual targets for thwacking deafeningly—
while hunting for food, digging out their homes,
seeking mates, and proclaiming their kingdoms—
provide opportunities for louder noise making.
Woodpeckers tend to use these items of convenience
after they have satisfied their other needs.
Then they use a variety of feeding methods
to locate available food.
Sometimes they search visually, digging—
starting at the base of a tree
and slowly working their way up,
constantly looking into every cranny for hiding insects.
They flip over chunks of bark to reveal concealed bugs,
or dig their way deep into the core of the tree
with their strong beaks to reach the succulent larvae.
It is at this point that the loud drumming
on the exterior of houses
and the resulting damage ceases—
much to the relief of Cape homeowners.

The Best Cape Cod Summer
In 50 Years

From several important perspectives,
the summer of 2010 was the finest I have seen.
The weather was nearly perfect—
day after day of warming and tanning sun,
reasonable temperatures, low humidity,
refreshing sea breezes, and cloudless skies—
ideal beach (or fun) days.
Of course there were some days
when temperatures and humidity soared,
but they were infrequent
and never approached the level reached off-Cape
in the rest of New England.
Temperatures there reached the high nineties
(heat waves) and humidity levels were oppressive,
with dew points in the mid-sixties.
From the standpoint of business
in this scenic destination vacation peninsula,
where success is measured in dollars,
hotel and motel occupancy rates,
restaurant receipts, and other types of sales,
commerce flourished.
The Cape probably sunk two feet
into Nantucket Sound and Cape Cod Bay
due to the weight of the visitors.
The main negative was traffic congestion.
Main roads, such as Routes 28 and 6A,
developed stop-and-go conditions and resembled
parking lots at certain times of day and evening.
Yet, all in all, it was a very good summer,
unquestionably one of the very best in years.

Tornado

On June 10, 2011, at least two confirmed tornadoes
descended upon the city of Springfield
and several other western Massachusetts towns,
moving from West to East over several hours.
The twister left four dead,
hundreds injured, many seriously.
It smashed homes and buildings, toppled trees
and scattered debris
across a 40-mile stretch of countryside.
Although not as common in New England
as they are in the Midwest and South,
we see, on average, two or three tornadoes per year,
I remember well the terrible death and damage
caused by the twister that hit Worcester
on Wednesday, June 10, 1953:
94 people killed, 1,288 injured, 10,000 left homeless.
and $52 million in damages,
including 4,000 buildings and hundreds of cars.
We were living in Ashby that year,
but I saw the appalling destruction left in its wake
in a visit to the city a few days later.

Life

Don't live with regrets
Fix the emotive damage
By self-forgiveness

Elicited Memories

What reminds you of a past romance?
For many, it is a song, photo, movie, or holiday.
For others, it is a letter, poem, specific place,
birthday, or date.
For me, it's the scent of the popular perfume,
Prince Matchebelli's Windsong,
worn by a girl I loved intensely many years ago.
The identical experience has been repeated
multiple times over many years—
and invariably with highly emotional results.
Swiftly, I am transported to that romantic era,
when I was so very young,
highly impressionable, and so much in love.

Here's how the exhilarating event now happens:
Suddenly and without warning,
a subtle cloud of perfume,
raised by a passing woman,
elicits breathtaking memories of my long-ago love.
The episode is always totally unexpected,
and unstoppable—
simultaneously powerful and unnerving,
but also exciting and intriguing.
The affects are so welcome that I deliberately
invited them several years ago
by buying the perfume for my wife,
and more recently, for my lover.
The effect is also available
simply by saying "Windsong."

———————

Introduced by design house Prince Matchabelli, Windsong
perfume has the scent of florals with fruity, green middle
notes, finishing with hints of musk and amber. It is
recommended for casual evening use.

The Women in My Life

I'm a very lucky man. I have had two mothers,
Pauline, my birth mother, and her sister, Josephine,
who nurtured me and brought me to adulthood
when my mother died in childbirth.
In addition to my two daughters,
Kathy and Maura,
I have eight granddaughters,
Tamra, Jackie, Mikie, Laine,
Katie, Kolby, Kaylyn, and Siara,
two great granddaughters,
Kaila and Grace,
two daughters-in-law. Joanne, and Lina,
one grand daughter-in-law, Leah.
and six ex-daughters-in-law,
Susan, Janet, Kimberly, Janice, Kathy, and Linda.
I also had or have many other women in my life:
My wife, Kathleen, in Heaven,
Else-Marie, my lifeline and friend forever,
and Doris, Mary, Janet, Jane, Jean, Bernadette,
Lucille, Kathleen, Helen-Lou,
Jeanne, Martha, Annabel, Elizabeth, Norma,
Margaret, Stephanie, Judith, Mary, and Marie,
my current or long-ago, long-time friends,
and my professional associates,
Gertrude, Rachel, and Signe.
And then there were my administrative assistants,
sequentially over a 25-year period,
Irene, Nina, Myra, Ruth, and Sofia.
All of these women have touched my life
in important ways.

They have made me more sensitive,
more caring, more loving,
as well as more effective and productive
as a person, a teacher, and a manager.
They have given me far more
than I have given them.
I shall be eternally grateful
for their affection, understanding,
helpfulness,
thoughtfulness, and support.

Haiku

There are two key times
When men don't fathom women
Pre and post marriage

A true bachelor:
A man who has never made
The same mistake once.

A lovely woman
Is the first choice of a mate
For a homely man

A very plain girl
Oftentimes becomes the bride
Of a handsome man

A charming woman
Is a priceless gift from God
To men in great need

Nurses and Hospitals

They come in all colors, nationalities, ages,
shapes, sizes, degrees of comeliness, and sexes.
But the great majority of nurses are
true angels of mercy, help, and concern.
Some are outgoing, some are bubbly,
some are stern, all business,
some are reserved, even taciturn,
while a few are gregarious and outgoing,
eager to learn about the experiences
and background of their patients.
So the best nurses are always welcome visitors,
even those who appear at 0200 or 0500,
just before the end of their shifts
to draw blood or just to check your vital signs.
Sometimes they must subject you to indignities,
such as a female nurse inserting or removing
a Foley catheter, administering an in-bed sponge bath,
or assisting you to visit the latrine.
But even the visits to the toilet
are more than an aggravation
because they often involve pushing an IV stand

with its dispensing machine, bags of medications,
and plastic tubing hanging ahead of you
from the hospital bed to the inner sanctum,
where inevitably there is not enough space
to do your chores comfortably.
And, if you've never attempted to perform
the sponge bath and shaving routines
in a small hospital bathroom
while hooked up to an IV,
you've really missed a gigantic challenge.
All too often, even when your hospital room
is some distance from the nurses station,
the staffers on shift are completely oblivious
to the noise they create by opening
and closing the door to the secure medication
storage room, the nursing staff's break room and toilet,
or simply their conversations,
which are often accompanied by much laugher.
It's no wonder that most people
can't wait to be discharged
and sent home to recover from their visit
to even the best and most prestigious hospitals,
such as the Massachusetts General Hospital in Boston.

The Doctor-Patient Relationship

The bond between a physician and a patient
is crucial to both parties
because the investment of time, talent,
and emotion is substantial and essential
to the success of the patient's healthcare outcomes.
It is also crucial to the physician's reputation.
For many years, I have viewed myself as a partner
of the dozens of medical and dental professionals
who have collaborated with me
in finding solutions to a variety
of medical and dental issues and problems.
In fact, I have sometimes been an aggressive partner
when I believe that I need to be more forceful.
It is also apparent that the attitudes
and actions of a physician's staff
often emphasize the primacy of the leader
of the practice
and seize every possible opportunity
to protect him or her from what they consider
to be overly vigorous and independent patient
actions or opinions.

Unfortunately, a practitioner's philosophy
is too often totally consistent
with earlier cultural norms,
which viewed patients primarily
as recipients and passive observers
of the medical and dental services provided to them
by highly-trained and experienced physicians.
It is also likely that the mentors of young physicians
in medical school and during internship
and residency assignments
emphasized by example the importance
of taking and remaining "in charge."
In recent years, as I reached my seventies and eighties,
the number of healthcare providers
that viewed their relationship with me as a partnership
declined and often became similar to the link
between a father and a young son—
perhaps indicating a belief
that senility had deprived me of the ability
to participate in any meaningful way
in healthcare discussions and decisions.
That is a judgment that should not be made
either lightly or often, if ever.

My Summer at the Farm

I worked on my grandfather's farm in 1939.
It was located in Northern New York state,
within walking distance of the Canadian border.
No electricity, no radio or TV, no phone, no bathroom.
No gas stove—only a woodstove for heat and cooking.

Sharing share a bed with my blind uncle, Ed.
Exchanging hilarious stories with him,
setting off laughter that always triggered a grouchy
bellow of "stop your noise and go to sleep,"
preceded by a thunderous bang
on the wall separating our room from Grandpa's.

Arising at 0500 every morning
and taking my turn in the outhouse
with uncle Ed, my sweet grandmother, Minnie,
and my gruff grandfather, Napoleon.
Milking six of the herd of 24 cows morning and night,
Uncle Ed and Grandpa dividing the remaining 18.

In the early morning, driving old Cliff down
to the Ellenburg train station
in the old wagon filled with six of seven
giant cans of milk.
Sharing the ride with Uncle Ed.

Returning to the old log house for a huge breakfast:
strong hot coffee, cereal with whole milk, eggs.
Canadian bacon, thick slices of homemade bread,
lathered with any one of five kinds of honey
from the hives kept by my beekeeper Grandpa.

Especially enjoyed—the mixture of sweet buckwheat
or clover honey spooned from the wooden boxes
along with the honey-filled wax cells
produced by the bees.
The meal always included pie for desert—
apple, blueberry, squash, or custard.

Breakfast was followed by work in the fields:
loading the hay wagon mowed two days earlier
and storing it in the barn.
It was hot work in July and August,
so our thirst was quenched by "ginger water"
ice cold well water, laced with dry ginger powder
—to prevent cramps.
At the end of the workday, swimming
in the icy cold water
of the creek that flowed through the farm
was a daily ritual.

The treat of the week occurred every Saturday
night in the old town hall—the weekly hoe down,
dancing, accompanied by accordion, flute, fiddle,
and some kind of percussion instrument,
such as drums, washboard, spoons, or bongos.

The girls, regardless of age, shape, or size,
were never without a dancing partner.
The upshot: wholesome, innocent,
enjoyable and satisfying fun.
I took full advantage of those occasions,
and the opportunities for socializing they unlocked,
whenever I had transportation and time.

A Message for My Children

If there were only one message I could leave
I'd try my very best to help you see
That you're the primary reason I live my life
and how much you mean to me.

Beginning the day you came into this world.
and I held you in my arms,
I realized that my purpose on this earth
Was to keep you safe from harm.

There was a place inside of me,
A place that I couldn't see
I had an emptiness inside
A feeling I just couldn't hide.

Although you may not have always understood
The ways that I behaved
All the paths that I have taken
Were attempts your life to save.

Take time for your children
Every day show them how much you love them
Always listen to their special needs
Praise them even when they stray,
And they will always come back your way.

Haiku

Wanting to live long
To enjoy some intervals
Of real happiness

A Poet's Wish

I'd really love to see my verses
in books that people read,
On pages they could turn to
whenever they feel the need.
Verses so powerful they would touch the heart
And maybe even excite the mind.
With every enthusiastic reader
Telling friends about their find.

What more could a would-be poet ask?
Than to be affluent and famous
And receive recognition in which to bask.

Yes I'd like to see
my verses inside books
So that whenever I have a need for affirmation,
I could quickly take a look.

So, to the reader of this doggerel
I hope there's no confusion
Getting my verse inside a book
Is always an auspicious conclusion.

Haiku

Life is beautiful
Death is irrevocable
Which one do you choose?

At Christmas Time 2009

The end of the year is rapidly approaching.
The days remaining include Christmas,
the annual Tracey Family Christmas Party,
and my 87th birthday.
It also marks the 12th year and
Christmas with Else-Marie in my life,
an anniversary well worth celebrating
because those years have given me the love
and companionship I needed so badly.
Else-Marie has been a blessing
that I did not earn and did nothing to deserve,
but I accept them with gratitude and jubilation.
My health has been problematic for much of the year
as evidenced by 23 visits to five physicians,
multiple diagnostic tests, including nuclear
and chemical stress, pulmonary function.
carotid ultrasound, echocardiogram,
and peripheral vascular tests, chest x-rays,
CT-scan, and multi-panel blood tests.
I have had 20 C-Lab blood drawings, seven phone
and two office pacemaker checks,

and six dental appointments.
Despite those health setbacks, I have had the blessing
of another year of love and companionship.
Never doubt for a moment how much
that has meant to me,
and will always mean to me, to have Else-Marie
as a friend and companion.
There's a special sort of feeling
that's warm and loving,
a special kind of warmth, that comes
with every thought of her.
Whatever makes her sad, whatever makes her glad,
to her Bill matter greatly.
I hope and pray nightly that many happy days
are yet to come
for her, for me, and whomever else she chooses.
And she should always remember this:
Even when words are not spoken or written,
my love for her is always in my heart.
So, these special thoughts on this day
are full of hugs for her
to let her know how much she is loved
all year through.

Images

Please don't ask me what I'm thinking
because you will not understand
that there are images in my mind
that I can't obliterate.
No one can grasp the pain of the question
that keeps my heart so sad.
Although I have tried to repress
the memories that obsess me,
the images persist unchanged.
I often pray that those icons
will disappear.
And I try to see the positives
to mitigate the ache,
hoping that I can learn something
from the distress of the ordeal.
Lord, remove these images from my mind
and help me to see the light
that must be shining on the other side
of this dark and dreary night.

The Entertaining Arts

Exciting and challenging!
Sometimes highly remunerative,
but, it's a rough life: keenly competitive,
involving constant travel,
and essentially a nomadic existence.
Its characteristics?
Difficulty maintaining spousal relationships,
frequent temptations or destructive addictions,
financial uncertainty and insecurity
dependence on agents,
inconsistent and self-centered managers,
and unpredictable club owners.
Also imperious and aggressive unions,
differing priorities of supporters, no guarantees
beyond scheduled and contracted engagements,
and the nightly challenge of a new audience.
In short, it is a profession fraught with risk,
nonetheless yielding rewards,
not just or primarily financial,
but also intrinsically
emotive and expressive.

Outpatient Surgery

Arising at 0500, before sunrise
on a beautiful late July summer day,
boasting 70 degrees with no humidity.
Shaving and entering the outside shower,
my daily habit and indulgence.
Dressing comfortably in shorts, golf shirt,
and new sandals.
Watching Else-Marie repeat the ritual visit
to the outside shower.
Upon returning from the shower,
wrapped in a towel,
she stood before me and proudly and unashamedly
dropped the towel and, with a shy smile,
revealed her lovely breasts,
the left breast showing the scar
of her lumpectomy done 20 years earlier.
Now with great courage facing a repeat surgery,
having adamantly refused to undergo
the radical mastectomy
recommended by her surgeon.
With love and compassion, she decided
to spare herself and me,
the trauma of that disfigurement.
Arriving at the hospital at 0615,
with parking close by and plentiful,
she signed in at the outpatient surgery desk.
Waiting patiently for admission
to the pre-op waiting area,
announced by a revolving color-coded chart
with entries beside each ID number,
the surgeon's name, and a notation
(CC Pre-op Bay 09)

announcing the readiness of the patient
to receive family.
Getting directions to the waiting area
and being met on the way by a male nurse,
who announced that Else-Marie
was to go immediately
to Pre-Op for preliminary surgical preparations.
Seeing her being seated in a wheelchair
and after receiving a kiss and a hug,
I left, having been told that I would receive
a phone call at home following the surgery.
Receiving the impatiently-awaited call
from the surgeon at 1030,
relieved to hear that the surgery had gone well
and that laboratory examination
provided negative results
relating to her underarm lymph nodes.
I returned to the hospital at 1130 and,
after a short wait, I met a very chipper
and much relieved Else-Marie.
I drove home with one important stop:
A Hess convenience store
to purchase Else-Marie's daily numbers.
All in all, it was a very good day!

Haiku

EMB is cool
Because she has a big heart
And cares totally

A great rarity
An understanding woman
—and a gift from God

The Depression at Christmas

The '30s were difficult years.
Sometimes, Pop had a plumbing job.
Other years he didn't have work.
But, we always looked forward to Christmas.

We always had a decorated tree,
using the same lights and treasured ornaments
of former years, including the angel
at the top of the tree and the tinsel,
which had been carefully removed
and stored before the tree was taken
to the dump the year before.
Of course the tree itself had been cut in the woods,
or purchased the week before Christmas
at a much reduced price
because it was not well shaped.
It typically required makeshift limbs
attached with wire and/or tape
where needed to fill the gaps in its foliage.

Of course, stockings were hung
behind the dining room stove
because we had no fireplace.
Late on Christmas Eve,
Mom filled the two stockings
with oranges (and apples from the supply in the cellar
harvested in the fall from our own trees)
red-striped candy canes, a small chocolate Santa Clause,
and a few inexpensive trinkets
purchased from the Five-and Ten,
such as little cars or dolls,
puzzles, jacks or yo-yos.

Presents under the tree were few:
mostly clothing, sometimes hand-me-downs
sent to us by our wealthy Connecticut cousins.
For my sister, Eileen, there was often a doll
or some other girl's gift,
and (rarely) for me a big gift,
such as a pair of inexpensive skiis
or on one Christmas, a Flexible Flier sled.
Always there was one special gift—a boy's book.
either a Hardy Boy (*The Sinister Sign Post,*
The Tower Treasure, or *The Secret of the Old Mill;*
a Horatio Alger book, such as *Do and Dare,*
Making His Way, Brave and Bold,
or one of the Tom Swift books,
such as *Tom Swift and His Motor Cycle,*
and His Big Dirigible, and His Air Glider, . . .
or *. . . and His Wireless Messages.*
For me, the annual gift book was the best present.

Dinner was invariable a roasted stuffed chicken
from our own chicken coop
with home grown (mashed) potatoes and gravy,
Hubbard or butternut squash, green beans, hot rolls,
cranberry sauce, and desert—apple, squash,
or custard pie.
It was always a great feast, even though
the larder was nearly bare for the rest of the week.

Fortunately, neither my sister Eileen nor I
ever realized we were poorer than our neighbors
on Washington Street's eastern end
near the Leominster Hospital.
And actually we fared far better
than many children in other parts of the city.

Sobriety

An addiction to alcohol
invariably and inevitably adversely effects
and often also terminates a life.
I have watched the terminal effect three times.
In each case, over a period of years
three people who were close to me:
my brother, Jack, my foster father, Eddie,
and my father-in-law, Tom, succumbed
to that terrible disease
They were at one time, bright, personable,
productive, and fun to be with—happy people!
But they died despondent, painfully,
and in two cases in an institution,
And in the other case, he died completely alone.
My experience with alcohol was quite different.
For many years, I either chose not
to drink alcohol in any form
or drank only occasionally and moderately,
fearing that I would become the inebriated person
my foster father became almost nightly.
Over time, I developed the habit of imbibing daily

my happy hour—at home, the local bar,
the officers' club, or the home of a colleague.
Drinking became a routine, an addiction,
although I was fortunate
that it did not adversely affect
my on-the-job behavior or professional competence.
Unfortunately, it began to affect my health,
resulting in gastric problems, including severe pain
and hospitalization for acute pancreatitis.
I was told by my gastroenterologist that continued
use of alcohol could exacerbate the condition
and result in death.
The hospitalization episode was ended (or cured)
by a laparoscopic cholecystectomy
(removal of the gall bladder).
Luckily, the surgery also resulted
in my embracing sobriety.
I stopped drinking alcohol in any form,
whether beer, wine, or spirits, January 4. 2004.
I have not had an alcoholic drink since.
As a consequence, a new life not only beckoned
but also became a reality
Thanks be to God!

The Plumber's Gofer

Occurring during the late 1930's,
during the Great Depression.
Having attained the age of fifteen,
I was eligible to serve as a plumber's helper
for my foster father, Eddie Tracey.

Arising during the summer
and weekends at 0630.
Arriving at the worksite in Leominster,
Clinton, or Fitchburg before 0800.
Performing routine plumbing tasks
such as cutting and threading brass
or galvanized pipe.

Caulking soil pipe joints,
using oakum, hot lead, a hammer
and a cold chisel.
Re-caulking the leaky joints,
following the plumbing inspector's test.
Filling the soil pipe with water
until it flowed over the roof.
and rechecking all joints for leaks.
Doing other gofer-type tasks.

Gradually learning and performing
more complex plumbing tasks,
such as cutting galvanized and brass pipes
to the proper length, threading pipes
to connect with elbows, forty-fives,
unions, couplings,
toilet and sink fixtures, and shut-offs.

Eating lunch at noon—
a sandwich, a cup of hot cocoa from the thermos
(or lemonade in the summer),
an apple, a banana, even apiece of homemade
cake, pie, or a doughnut for dessert.

On bad days, cleaning up after the carpenters,
who mindlessly used the toilet
regardless of the fact that
it couldn't be flushed—
leaving a stinking mess
that had to be dipped out
using a tin can—my job!

Quitting work at 1700
and riding or driving to Leominster.
Parking at the railroad station
while Pop walked the tracks
to the Blue Moon Saloon
for a couple of dime beers—
and stopping on the way back to the car
to buy a nickel ice cream cone,
my only pay for the day's work.

Riding or driving home for a sumptuous dinner
prepared by my foster mother, Josephine.
That was my daily routine
during the summers of 1936 through 1939.

That was my routine
for all of my summers during junior high
and high school.

A Delayed College Enrollment

In May 1940, I was asked to remain after class
by Mrs. Manning Morrill, my English teacher.
Wondering what kind of trouble I was in
so close to graduation, I reported as ordered.
Surprised by her first question:
"Do you plan to apply for college entrance?"
Immediately responding:
"No. I'm graduating from the General Course,
instead of the College Preparatory Course—
which makes me ineligible for college entrance."
Startled by her response:
"I believe that you can and should apply
and your Principal, Mr. Davis and I
will recommend your admission."
In my wildest dreams, I never believed
that I would be accepted at any college.
Yet, I ran all the way home to report
the discussion with my foster mother.
She was more than pleased;
she was enthusiastic and thrilled.
We discussed the possibilities and soon determined
that Fitchburg State Teachers College
was the obvious choice
because the college was only a trolley ride away,
would not require dormitory
or dining accommodations,
tuition and fees were inexpensive
and offered a program in secondary education.
I applied immediately,
and was accepted for enrollment
in the Class of 1944.

Then came the fateful reaction and decision
of my foster father, Eddie Tracey.
He was enraged by my enrollment,
told me that I could not attend
and must cancel my enrollment.
He informed me that it was "pay-back time"
for the many years he had supported me.
I was devastated.
But my mother took me aside, and said,
"I know how disappointed you are, but do as he said.
I promise that it will only postpone your enrollment.
You will be enrolled next year.
So let's prepare for that reality."
I found a 25 cents per hour laborer's job
at the Whitney Reed Company unloading freight cars
and performing similar unskilled labor jobs
until there was an opening
at the Cluett and Peabody Shirt Company
for a shortage chaser
(locating misplaced shirt parts)
that paid 30 cents per hour,
The $12 weekly income was divided as follows:
$5 for board and room, $5 banked for college tuition,
and $2 for spending money.
As September approached, I was given a parting gift
by the 300 piece-work ladies
at Cluett and Peabody
(enough to cover the first year's
tuition and books at FSTC).
I reapplied for enrollment in the Class of 1945,
was accepted. and Pop Tracey raised no objections,
no doubt due my foster mother's insistence.
Thus began my academic career.

Christmas Morning

Awakening groggily
to the patter of little feet
and the plunks of sleepy teenagers
on their way to the family room at 5 A.M.
Racing down the staircase to join them.
Seeing the six children
waiting impatiently for their mother
to join the eager flock.
Having grabbed their stockings,
on their way past the kitchen fireplace,
filled with oranges, candy, bubble gum
and trinkets,
such as jacks, marbles, scout knives,
and slinkys.
Seeing the sadly unbalanced
but lighted Christmas tree decorated
with colorfully wrapped presents
arranged beneath
and the larger unwrapped toys—
baby carriage, scooter,
tricycle, skis, and train set
that I had laboriously assembled
from eleven P.M. until two A.M.
Listening contentedly to the oohs and ahas
as each gift was unwrapped.
And outside seeing a wonderland
of ice-glazed trees all diamond-spiked
with bowl-shaped limbs
filled with white frosty stems
mirroring a rainbow hue of sunrise glow,
and that warm feeling of happiness
to have such a wonderful family.

My Prescription for Loneliness

People fantasize because they are unhappy.
People write letters because they are alone.
People make phone calls because
they are depressed.
People visit friends and acquaintances
because they are lonely.
People seek love because they need affection.
All of these actions are cries for help,
appeals for nurture, support, and comfort.
Psychiatrists tell us that all humans
need companionship, contact with others,
caring, affection, and love
just as much as they need food.
Denied the fulfillment of those needs
for a prolonged period
people become physically ill.
Some become clinically depressed,
unable to deal with the vicissitudes of life.
So, if you are afflicted with loneliness,
do what you must do to preserve your sanity.
You have many options!

Our Honeymoon

Remembering the first day of July 1944.
Departing 326 Lunenburg Street
the home of my bride, Kathleen,
where we had just enjoyed
our wedding reception in the barn
with about 30 family members and friends.
Leaving for the bus station in Fitchburg
in Uncle Cecil's 1938 Chevrolet four-door sedan
for the honeymoon trip to Boston.

Embarrassed by the clatter and jangle
caused by the tin cans on strings
attached to the car's rear bumper
bouncing along Lunenburg Street, Moran Square,
and lower Main Street.
Enduring the amused faces of pedestrians
as the noisy car passed by.

Boarding the bus at the bus station.
Sitting beside the bride in the wide back seat,
a newly commissioned Naval ensign
and a brand new husband.
Carrying a bankroll amounting to $38.00,
just enough to cover one night in a hotel
and one inexpensive evening meal.
Arriving at Park Square in the late afternoon.
Taking a taxi from the bus station
to the hotel entrance,
which we discovered
to our dismay and embarrassment,
and the cabdriver's amusement,

was just around the corner.
Registering for the first time as
Ensign and Mrs. William R. Tracey
Later, walking to dinner to a nearby cafeteria,
where the food was inexpensive
but not memorable.

Encountering a Navy enlisted man
in his white summer uniform.
on our way back to the hotel.
Receiving and returning my first salute
as a commissioned officer
—and stopping the sailor to give him
the traditional reward of one dollar
for that memorable salute.

Reentering our hotel room anxious
and nervous about the first-time pleasures
I assumed awaited me
—but were not experienced on that occasion
for reasons that are not uncommon,
but best left to the reader's imagination.

The next day we took the subway
to my sister Pauline's apartment in the Roxbury
Project near the Mission Church
where we spent the next few days and nights
before returning to Fitchburg for one night.
Riding again in the Chevrolet driven
by Uncle Cecil to the Worcester train station.
Leaving by train for San Francisco
and duty in the Pacific Theater
with my bride crying softly on the platform
and waving to me through her tears.

A Speech Malady

Unfortunately, millions of English-speaking
Americans of all races, nationalities, educational
levels, and professions
are the victims of an omnipresent affliction
formally called the "vocalized pause."
Its most frequent and most annoying symptom
is the all too familiar "you know,"
often used several times in the same utterance.
Other examples include "ah," "er." "uh," "um,"
"I mean," "aannddss," "uuuhhs,"
and "it's-it's-it's-it's" in rapid succession.
Three prominent sufferers of the malady are
Robert Gibbs, White House Press Secretary,
a knowledgeable and experienced political strategist
familiar with President Obama's
political goals and objectives.
His favorite interjections, used to fill in long pauses,
are "aannddss" or "uuuhhs."
Caroline Kennedy Schlossberg,
a graduate of Radcliffe College (Harvard)
and Columbia Law School.
and a well-known writer and editor,
used "you know"142 times in one interview.
Martha MacCallum of TV's Fox News,
the well informed, brainy, and articulate
on-camera personality, whose burden is also
the overuse of "you know" exclusively in unscripted
comments and discussions.
These are only a sample of the millions
of Americans who suffer the contagious disease
of vocalized pauses.

Agonizing

Placing daily phone calls
to my best friend.
Reaching only her voice mail.
Promising to "call me back."
Despairing because there were
no return calls.

Worrying about her welfare.
Questioning her whereabouts.
Wondering what is going on.
Brooding over her failure
to keep her promise
to stay in touch.

Dreading to be abandoned.
Struggling to keep my composure.
Wrestling with uncertainty.
Anguishing about my concern.
Fearing a negative call.

Entreating God's assistance.
Petitioning for the help of Saint Jude.
Feeling reprieved by a
single message on my voice mail—
a warm and positive transmission.
Restoring my faith in my friend.

I Regret

The times that I failed
to be caring.
The days that I wasn't forgiving.
The lost opportunities
to be understanding.
The weeks I was
away from home.
The years that passed
so swiftly.
If only I had done the things
that I now know
that I should have done—
and wish that I had.
But now the time has passed.
It is too late except
to hope and pray
that I am forgiven.

Haiku

Talk less than your spouse
Listen much more than you talk
You'll learn more that way

Four o'clock habit
A very dry Martini
Nectar of the Gods

Living alone sucks
What can be done about it?
Find a companion

Our Ordeal

Waiting impatiently for your arrival from work.
Seeing your car turn into the driveway.
Expecting your entry into the living room
Anticipating a hug and a kiss.
Sensing that all was not right.
Peering out the window.
Catching a glimpse of you prone on the asphalt walk.

Rushing out to you with great trepidation.
Attempting to get you up on your feet.
Realizing that you were badly hurt.
Knowing that you had to get out of the frigid air.
Wishing that I could lift you in my arms.
Recognizing that I could not do so.
Encouraging you to pull yourself into the house.
Watching your courageous and painful travail.

Believing that I should call 911 immediately.
Postponing that action at your insistence.
Bandaging your wounded and bleeding knee.
Fulfilling your need for nourishment with a salad.
Facing the problem of moving you to the bathroom.
Agreeing that it was an impossibility.

Making the 911 call for help.
Feeling completely helpless and useless.
Wanting desperately to comfort and sustain you.
Marveling at your fortitude and composure.
Seeing the departure of the ambulance for the hospital.
Needing to be with you.
Perceiving that I should stay at home.

Spending a long night awaiting your call.
Feeling much relieved when you contacted me.
Quivering with emotion when informed
that your hip was fractured.
Lying awake for hours.
Praying intermittently for the Lord's
(and Saint Jude Thaddeus') help.
Expecting, with deep concern
that you were in surgery.
Noting that the suspense was over
when Dr. Smith, your surgeon, called.
Informing me that the operation
was successfully completed at 1700 hours.
Acknowledging again my admiration
and love for you.
Recognizing anew that
it takes fortitude, endurance, and will power
to be the kind of woman you are.
Never doubt for a second
how much it has meant to me
to have you as my friend and companion.
The years we have been together
have been blessings that I did not earn or deserve.

Haiku

Stock your memories
Learning outstrips forgetting
You'll keep more that way

Loving is risky
But it also yields rewards
The greatest—shared love.

Counting My Blessings

My heritage—born into a loving and industrious
Irish, French Canadian and American Indian family,
   all members having great promise and potential.
My up-bringing—being loved, cherished, and reared
   by Josephine, first as my aunt when I was a child,
   and later, when she became my adoptive mother.
My siblings—Although living separated for many
         of our childhood and young adult years,
      we lived across the street for several years
      and never lost close and continuing contact
         with each other until separated by death.
   My early education—which was valued,
   encouraged and supported by my foster mother
      despite obstacles raised by my foster father.
   My professional education—encompassing
      college, graduate school, and postgraduate
         education and training, supported by
   the Federal government, the Navy, and the Army.
   My wife, Kathleen—my best friend, companion,
      helpmate, supporter, lover, and the mother
               of our six children.
   My children—every one of them loving, gifted
      in different ways, innovative, independent,
            entrepreneurial, and successful.
      My friends—Most of them now deceased,
but all played important supporting roles in my life
      a few from childhood and early adulthood,
   others during college and graduate school years,
      and still others in the last 25 or more years.
            I have been blessed!

Identifying My Challenges

Making lifestyle adjustments to accommodate
the demands of an aging body and mind.
Accepting limitations on my ability
to continue starting and completing
minor home repair and maintenance jobs.
Keeping track of medical, dental, and lab visits
and daily doses of prescription medicines
and vitamin supplements to preserve
and improve my health.
Adjusting to the deaths of family, relatives
and friends due to age, illness, or accident.
Avoiding time in the sun due to the danger
of sun caused basal and squamous cell
carcinomas and the dreaded melanoma.
Needing to discontinue bicycle riding
due to the danger of falling while taking
a daily dose of "blood-thinning" Warfarin.
Dealing with the increasing need
for medical, dental, lab, and pharmacy visits,
to maintain my health and well being.
Limiting driving distances and time of day
behind the wheel to compensate
for age-related reduced reaction time.
Tolerating momentary lapses in memory,
such as searching for the right words
and remembering names and dates.
Accepting the inevitability of death—
lucky to still be here—
as I approach the age of 89,
living this way for a time
or welcoming the alterative sooner.

Noteworthy Events of 2010

On Jan 12, after more than 25 years
with my good friend and primary care physician,
Dr. Nile N. Albright, due to travel limitations.
with great reluctance, I discontinued
my semiannual trips to Boston
and engaged Paul H. Cochrane, D.O. of Cape Cod
as my primary health provider.
Jan 30 I attended son Sean's 50th birthday party
at the Red Door in Portsmouth, NH.
I read a special verse celebrating his professional
and family accomplishments
14 Feb, I started a 30-minute daily exercise bike
regimen that lasted about six months,
at which time I was unable to continue the exercise
due to peripheral artery disease.
18 Mar marked my last appointment with (retiring)
John W. tenBroeke. M.D., my cardiologist for 12 years,
and engaged Luke F. Daley, M.D. as his replacement.
13 April Oliver Kelly Roofing installed a new roof
on my house, bunkhouse, and equipment shed.
15 April Maura began to move in with me on Cape.
15 Jun Maura retired from her teaching position
in Rome, NY where Kevin read a verse
that I wrote for the occasion.
7 Jul Bill Jr. celebrated his 63rd birthday
10 Jul my last surviving sibling, my sister Peg,
died in a nursing home.
Her funeral was held July 13th in Needham
with burial in Waltham next to 2nd husband, Joe Natale.
28 Aug my grandson (Kathy's son) Sean Keenan Letellier

married Leah Brandon in a ceremony on Dennisport beach,
followed by a reception at Leah's parent's cottage.
25 Oct Kevin and Brian celebrated their 62nd birthday.
30 Oct, the 13th anniversary of wife Kathleen's death,
was marked by a visit to her grave
at the National Cemetery in Borne,
an Anniversary Mass at St. Pius Tenth Church,
and a dinner at the Olympia Restaurant in South Yarmouth.
Nov 2, my third great grandchild and first great grandson,
David Matthew Munson, was born in Seattle, WA—
son of granddaughter Jackie and husband, Matt,
David weighed in at 8 lbs., 10 oz.
25 Nov We celebrated Thanksgiving dinner
at Kathy's in Hollis, NH.
18 Dec the family Christmas party was held
at my home in South Yarmouth.
29 Dec I celebrated my 88th birthday quietly
with Else-Marie
by going out to dinner at Doyle's Restaurant.

* * *

The year 2010 marked the demise
of the long-running Tracey Edwards Company,
the renowned, highly successful,
marketing, branding, and advertising corporation;
the sale of Kevin's favorite possession,
a twin-engine, pressurized, and well appointed
Piper Mojave corporate aircraft;
and the loss of his favorite toy,
a 48-foot sleek and luxurious sailboat,
the *Rhapsodie en Bleu.*
It also marked the birth of
Kevin Tracey Companies, LLC,
a new advertising, marketing, branding,
and social media consulting firm.
based in Manchester, New Hampshire.

*   *   *

The year was equally eventful for Brian—
with the profitable sale of his software firm, Estorian,
and the steady growth of his popular and lucrative
Ride-the-Ducks-of-Seattle tourist attraction.
The year also marked the purchase
of another yacht, the *Entertainer,* Gulfstar 60 Mark II,
outfitted with the latest navigational
and sailboat technology and all of the amenities
demanded by the opulently wealthy.

*   *   *

The year also marked the flowering
of Kevin' sprima terpsichoreans,
Kolby and Kaylyn Tracey,
his bright, talented, and lovely daughters.
It also signaled the sale of his Bedford property,
the construction and occupation
of a new condominium in Manchester,
and his renewed status as a bachelor.
And for Brian, 2010 not only traced
the maturation of the love of his senior years,
his first granddaughter Grace,
but also the conception of his second grandchild,
David Matthew Muson.

*   *   *

Bill Jr. accomplished something unique
for most families with boaters and sailors.
He passed the master's examination for captaining ships
that carry passengers—the Ph.D. of shipmasters,
whether engine or sail propelled,
and of men and women
who are qualified and certified marine pilots.

A Blessing

This blessing comes with love
Today and every day
To bring a special prayer
For my offspring often to replay.
May God light your life with grace
And keep you in His care.
May this day and every day
Be filled with joy and peace
From morning until night,
And may the years that lie ahead
Be especially glad and bright.

Index

As a boy I did
What my father demanded
When is it my turn?